Praise for *Creating a School Library with Impact*

'*Creating a School Library with Impact* is an essential toolkit for all those managing or working in a school library. Topics range from practical perennial issues such as stock selection, layout and control, to managing behaviour, information and digital literacy, and Equality, Diversity and Inclusion policies amongst others. With specific chapters relating to managing primary school libraries and CPD for librarians, this will serve as a useful guide for all school librarians.'
Judy Broady-Preston, Professor Emerita, Prifysgol Aberystwyth University and Editor, *Global Knowledge Memory and Communication (GKMC)*

'There has never been a more important time for every child in every school to have access to an outstanding school library. This deeply researched, highly practical book is a must-read for education leaders, librarians and all those concerned with young people's literacy.'
Dr Richard Gerver, President of the School Library Association

'This book is written by a team of amply experienced and qualified professionals, inspiring confidence in the reader from the very outset. A must read for those just beginning to establish themselves as school library professionals in the UK, it provides thoughtful consideration of how to create library environments that are calm, supportive of diversity, employing technology in productive ways, and conducive to learning and reading.

Key knowledge and skills to be learned in the library (such as digital literacy and academic integrity) are accompanied by vignettes that show how this can be enacted, and there are many practical tips that can be immediately added to the reader's existing repertoire. The result is a book that resonates with both expertise and practical value.'
Dr Margaret Merga, Merga Consulting and Honorary Adjunct at the University of Newcastle, Australia

'*Creating a School Library with Impact* provides a wealth of knowledge and information for those embarking on a career as a school librarian and is equally valuable for those already in the role aiming to enhance and rejuvenate their activities. It is acknowledged that libraries operate within an environment that is constantly changing and the team of contributing authors have covered a wide range of key topics from the strategic to the practical.

They are all experienced practitioners and this shows through in the guidance and encouragement provided, supported where appropriate with underpinning theory. As an LIS educator this book will be a valuable addition to module reading lists.'

Dr Carolynn Rankin, Associate Lecturer, School of Education, Ulster University and IFLA Libraries for Children and Young Adults Standing Committee Member

'Publications about school librarianship often focus on the functions of the school library and lose sight of the human component. What makes this book special is that while it provides necessary practical advice for school librarians to deal with materials, business requirements, working with students and more, it also reveals the principles of contemporary school librarianship – what gives meaning to the work of the school library. Reading is considered as not only an activity that enables the acquisition of information, but also as something that forms students by finding books that inspire and engage them.

Creating a School Library with Impact will be relevant for all school librarians who want to encourage reader development, set meaningful priorities and make the library the heart of the school. It is an excellent tool for both beginners and experienced librarians, who will find new incentives and inspiration for their work in the examples, scenarios and case studies.'

Dr Ivanka Stricevic, University Professor and Director General of the National and University Library, Zagreb, Croatia

Creating a School Library with Impact

Creating a School Library with Impact
A Beginner's Guide

Caroline Roche, Barbara Band,
Nick Cavender, Lucy Chambers,
Annie Everall, Ellen Krajewski and
Sarah Pavey

For the School Libraries Group of CILIP

facet
publishing

Published by Facet Publishing
7 Ridgmount Street, London WC1E 7AE
www.facetpublishing.co.uk

Facet Publishing is wholly owned by CILIP: the Library and Information Association.

British Library Cataloguing in Publication Data
A catalogue record for this book is available from the British Library.

ISBN 978-1-78330-553-7 (paperback)
ISBN 978-1-78330-554-4 (hardback)
ISBN 978-1-78330-555-1 (PDF)
ISBN 978-1-78330-556-8 (EPUB)

First published 2022

Text printed on FSC accredited material.

Typeset from authors' files by Flagholme Publishing Services in 10/13 pt Palatino Linotype and Open Sans.
Printed and made in Great Britain by CPI Group (UK) Ltd, Croydon, CR0 4YY.

Contents

Notes on Contributors

Caroline Roche

Caroline has worked in school libraries for around 30 years. She is passionate about creating exciting school libraries and about training school librarians to be excellent practitioners. Caroline was Chair of CILIP's School Libraries Group (SLG) for six years, ending her term in December 2022. She has also been Chair of the Great School Libraries campaign from its inception in 2019.

Barbara Band

Barbara is a qualified Chartered Librarian who, having worked for over 30 years in a wide range of school libraries within various sectors, now offers freelance consultancy, training and advice. She delivers customer-focused services to provide bespoke solutions, supported with project management skills gained in business and non-profit organisations. She also offers writing, reviewing and editing services. Barbara is currently Treasurer of the SLG and Chair of the Library Services Trust. A former CILIP Past President and Vice Chair of the Great School Libraries Campaign, she is passionate about the value and benefits that libraries can bring to schools.

Nick Cavender

Nick has been a school librarian for 15 years, having previously spent over a decade in the public library sector. Currently he is the librarian and extended projects co-ordinator at Rickmansworth School in Hertfordshire, where he is a keen advocate of digital literacy skills. Nick is treasurer of Herts School Library Association (SLA) and sits on the SLG committee as Vice Chair and Chair from January 2022.

Lucy Chambers

After many years as a primary school librarian and a former member of CILIP's SLG committee, Lucy now concentrates on children's books promotion and reviewing, writing about school librarianship, co-ordinating children's events and the children's poetry competition for the Chiswick Book Festival and advising on setting up, resourcing and managing primary school libraries. Lucy is also on the longlisting panel for the prestigious UKLA Book Award.

Annie Everall

Annie Everall OBE is Director of Authors Aloud UK, an agency organising author tours and visits to schools. A qualified librarian, she worked for Birmingham and Derbyshire Libraries where she developed a range of award-winning library services and initiatives. She is the Conference and Training Manager for CILIP's SLG and the Association of Senior Children's and Education Librarians (ASCEL). She is a Trustee for Read for Good and a member of the Federation of Children's Book Groups executive committee. She is a children's book reviewer, co-organiser of the Pupil Library Assistant of the Year Award and joint co-ordinator of the IFLA World Through Picture Books programme. She has presented keynotes at many UK and international conferences. In 2001, she was awarded the OBE for services to children's books and libraries.

Ellen Krajewski

Ellen spent her early career in retail and admin posts, devouring books on her daily commute. After having children, Ellen returned to work part-time, eventually securing a post in a college library. There, she had found her heaven and embarked on a distance learning Library & Information Studies degree with Aberystwyth University, graduating in 2011. Ellen worked in college and school libraries for 18 years until July 2019, when she took the opportunity to retire early and immediately launched into her first retirement project of total immersion in the Carnegie and Kate Greenaway (CKG) Medals! She has always been an avid reader and, as a child, spent her Saturday afternoons in the local public library. Ellen has a real passion for children's books and cross stitch, so if she hasn't got a book in her hand, she's listening to an audiobook while stitching. She has been actively involved in both CILIP's Youth Libraries Group (YLG) and SLG for some years and has also served three years on the board of SLA. Ellen had the privilege of being a CKG judge for the 2012, 2013 and 2016 medals and she feels greatly honoured to have been the Chair of Judges for the 2021 medals. She is currently Chair of YLG Eastern and also Chair of Herts SLA.

Sarah Pavey

Sarah works as an education consultant for her own company, SP4IL, having been a school librarian for over 20 years. She is a fellow of CILIP and RSA and is a committee member of both the SLG and the Information Literacy Group of CILIP. She co-authored *The Innovative School Librarian* and recently wrote *Playing Games in the School Library* for Facet Publishing.

Foreword

Professor Teresa Cremin, The Open University

School libraries and their skilled librarians deserve a higher profile. Far too often, the work they undertake, the opportunities they provide and the relationships they build with young learners remain under-appreciated and unacknowledged. They merit increased recognition and respect in our education system. For those teachers who are fortunate enough to work in schools with vibrant libraries and experienced librarians, their not inconsiderable value is evidenced on a daily basis. International research evidence affirms this, revealing that school libraries and librarians contribute to young people's literacy skills and attainment, their pleasure in reading and their wellbeing (e.g., Barratt, 2010; Williams, Wavell and Morrison, 2014).

In offering a brief Foreword at the start of this engaging and practical book, I focus on the ways in which school librarians nurture young people's reading for pleasure – their volitional reading. This contribution is crucial because it is now widely accepted that there is a reciprocal relationship between reading for pleasure and reading attainment (Sullivan and Brown, 2015; Chema, 2018). The will influences the skill and vice versa. Those young people, in primary or secondary schools, who are intrinsically motivated to read, and who choose to read for pleasure frequently and in their own time, will fly further and faster than their peers who do not. As Stanovich (1986) simply stated: 'Reading makes you smarter'.

Higher reading levels are not only associated with stronger academic outcomes, better employment and economic prospects (OECD, 2009), but are also associated with health benefits, including life expectancy and lower costs nationally (Billington, 2015; Boyes et al., 2016). Other benefits include wider general knowledge (e.g., Mar and Rain, 2015), enhanced imagination, empathy and mindfulness of others (e.g., Kidd and Costano, 2013) enriched narrative writing (Sénéchal, Hill and Malette, 2018), and new reader to reader relationships that can serve to create communities of readers (Cremin et al.,

2014). Thus, multiple personal, social and emotional benefits, as well as cognitive ones, accrue for those young people who choose to read. So, whilst the role of the school librarian encompasses far more than supporting the desire to read (within and beyond school), I would argue that nurturing reading for pleasure is the school librarian's primary responsibility. In what follows, I seek to share research that indicates the nature of the environment and the pedagogy needed to nurture young readers and reflect upon the positioning of school librarians.

Creating a reading for pleasure ethos and pedagogy

Whilst several studies have examined the benefits of volitional reading (e.g., McQuillan, 2019) and young people's declining attitudes to reading (e.g., Nootens et al., 2019), few have sought to document the environment and pedagogy that supports young readers and the ways in which librarians and teachers can build richly reciprocal reading communities that include all learners, particularly the less engaged or disadvantaged readers. However, the work of Ee Loh and colleagues in Singapore, my own work in England, Moses and Kelly's study in the US and Merga's research in Australia offer some useful insights in this regard.

In Singapore, drawing from a dataset of six secondary schools and their libraries, the research team collected data to help them understand the reading and school library culture. They documented the significant factors that shaped the success of the libraries and concluded there are five factors of importance, namely: designing effective reading spaces; curating the book selection; making books visible; producing programmes to engage and entice readers; and building an ecology for reading (Ee Loh et al., 2017). In relation to the last point, one library became a highly social and exciting space with students, teachers and the librarians engaged in a range of activities, not all of which were focused on reading (e.g., music workshops and poetry performances). The space was deliberately designed to entice readers to visit. The involvement of the principal, a keen reader himself, enhanced the engagement of all. Reading was recognised by the students in this school as part of their learning. They felt it was encouraged rather than enforced and many of them seized opportunities to read prior to morning assembly, in the library and in other spaces (Ee Loh et al., 2017).

In England, working with 27 primary schools, the *Teachers as Readers* study found that when the teachers widened their knowledge and pleasure in reading children's literature and other texts, and become more aware of their own and the children's reading practices, they began to reconceptualise reading from the inside out (Cremin et al., 2014). As a result, they were better positioned to build an effective reading for pleasure pedagogy and strong communities of readers in school. In some of the schools, librarians were central to this shift; in others, as is often the case in primary schools in England, the library was not staffed by trained librarians but by teaching assistants, parents and teachers. The research identified a coherent reading for pleasure pedagogy that encompassed planned time for reading aloud, for independent reading and for book talk, 'inside-text talk' and recommend- ations, all in the context of a social reading environment (Cremin et al., 2014).

In another UK-based study, the marked skill of secondary school librarians involved in supporting extracurricular reading groups was tracked (Cremin and Swann, 2017). The librarians leading these Carnegie and Kate Greenaway shadowing groups foregrounded reading choice (albeit limited to the shortlist), created a shared social space for reading (characterised by a lack of pressure) and offered rich opportunities to discuss the literary texts in an open dialogic manner. Relatively informal relationships were evident between leaders and group members and a relaxed stance towards reading was adopted by both the school librarians and the teachers in the groups. This effectively motivated the young readers, who noted the marked difference between reading in the group and reading during English lessons, where they perceived 'right answers' were expected and assessment was foregrounded (Cremin and Swann, 2017). In contrast, in the library environment there was considerable informality and less hierarchical relationships between the adults and the students. This, in the students' eyes, contributed to their positive dispositions towards reading during the extracurricular groups and at home.

In the United States, observing practice in one classroom of 6–7-year-olds, Moses and Kelly (2018, 2019) also found that when the teacher built a reading ecology in which reading became a socially shared endeavour, children chose to read. Their findings on the impact of the teacher's ethos and practice affirm the insights from Ee Loh et al. (2017) and Cremin et al. (2014). Despite the distinct age differences in the young people involved in these three studies, each reveal that adult text knowledge, book promotions and recommend- ations, alongside opportunities to hear texts read aloud, to read alone and with others and to discuss books in comfortable reading spaces are all essential elements of reading for pleasure pedagogy. They do not operate in isolation but combine in complex ways to nurture choice-led reading. These studies also connect to the strands identified by Mallette and Barone (2016) as the most impactful for developing young readers: time to read; access to books; and free choice of what to read.

In Australia, Merga (2017) explored what young people want to read and found that they reported not being able to find books that inspire and engage them. As a recent literature review of the impact and characteristics of school libraries and reading spaces recommends, 'there must be collaboration between pupils and school library staff to build collections of material that the children and young people (especially older pupils) want to read and are age appropriate and contemporary' (Rudkin and Wood, 2019, 16). A principled approach to selecting books must surely be deployed to ensure that the collection reflects the diverse realities of children's lives (Hartsfield and Kimmel, 2020). In another Australian study, teacher librarians worryingly reported that inadequate library resourcing was holding back the creation of a rich reading culture since the texts did not engage the young people (Merga and Mason, 2019). This has also been borne out by the recent National Literacy Trust report on the future of primary school libraries in the UK (Todd, 2021). Additionally, the Australian teacher-librarians expressed concern about the opportunities for time to read — they considered this a key strategy to support the development of keen readers, as previous studies have also indicated, but did not believe this was prioritised in their schools. This may have been a result of the limited influence of these librarians on the culture of reading for pleasure beyond the library.

The positioning of libraries and librarians

In some schools, shaped by history, politics and funding issues, libraries and librarians are somewhat marginalised. But in others, their distinctive value is recognised and their work is embraced by the English department, the staff team and the wider school leadership. When this is the case, the capacity of the library and the librarian to impact on young people's choice-led reading and life chances is significantly enhanced. Nonetheless, working in a culture of 'performativity' (Ball, 2000), underscored by narrow conceptualisations of reading as a set of cognitive skills, shapes the way many librarians are viewed and can constrain their influence on students' volitional reading. In England, reading for pleasure is mandated (DfE, 2014), but the timetable remains tight, budgets for books continue to be unreliable or small and library spaces are often encroached and used as meeting rooms, detention spaces or classrooms. Another challenge can be the use of digital library systems, which whilst they have the potential to position adults as co-readers, mentors and listeners, tend not to do so (Kucirkova and Cremin, 2017). The technological design of digital library systems needs to incorporate insights from research on reading pedagogy and reflect these to better support both librarians and teachers.

In responding to the dilemmas that librarians face, many work alongside teachers to embed reading for pleasure across the school, often co-teaching in classrooms and planning joint initiatives. As Aggleton, Carter and Grieve (forthcoming, 2022) note, 'librarians work across year groups, developing relationships with readers over many years, and can bring together not only children, but also staff, caregivers, and the local community to create truly reciprocal communities of readers'. Librarians seek to creatively involve staff from right across the school in diverse ways, widening teachers' knowledge of texts, engaging them as adult readers and enriching their understanding of the positive influence of reading for pleasure. In drawing the school staff into sharing their identities as readers with each other and the students, and offering engaging reading events, librarians can shift reading from being seen as a private pursuit to one that is recognised as a more collaborative social activity. Students and teachers will also contribute to the shaping of these reading events, negotiating and enacting their own relational identity positions as readers within them and getting to know each other and the adults as fellow readers. This offers strong support for young readers.

Conclusion

Given the continual decline in students' reading for pleasure in England (Clark and Teravainen-Goff, 2020), increased policy and practice recognition of the potential contribution of school librarians to this agenda is urgently needed. To nurture volitional reading and create a rich reading culture, school librarians need space, time, trust and decent budgets, as well as knowledge and understanding of the most effective ways forward. That is where this invaluable book comes in. Comprehensive and informed, written by colleagues with considerable experience and expertise, it encompasses attention to nurturing lifelong readers and many more aspects of the complex and exciting role of the school librarian. A rich cornucopia of ideas and practical strategies are offered that will enhance the personal and professional assurance of all who read it. Enjoy!

Preface

Caroline Roche and Nick Cavender

When I was approached by Facet Publishing, as Chair of the CILIP School Libraries Group (SLG), to see if we were interested in writing a book, I knew immediately what book I wanted us to produce – and it was this one. For years I had been passionate about training and CPD for school librarians. Whilst Chair of the SLG I had initiated training and projects, such as our Key Skills leaflets, to encourage people to grow and learn throughout their library careers.

One of the reasons I am so passionate about this is because of the way I began and continued my own career in school libraries. I myself had no formal library training – I still have neither a masters nor a degree in librarianship. When I started in school libraries, I had a degree in English and six years' experience behind the counter of a public library. At that time, I couldn't apply for Chartership. I was hungry to learn about my new job and as soon as CILIP opened up Chartership to people like me, I applied. I continued to seek out training courses, attend conferences and learn all about my library management system. I have been involved in lifelong learning ever since, taking a Masters in Education whilst working. I feel that if I can progress from knowing hardly anything about running a school library to being Chair of a wonderful group of professionals, then everyone else can too.

I do hope that you seize your own opportunity to learn everything you can from this book and that by the end you feel emboldened to carry on to become a Chartered Librarian as well. Even if you don't feel you want to do that, I hope that you continue learning and growing in this amazing profession of ours. Good luck to all of you!

Caroline Roche, MA, MCLIP. Chair of CILIPSLG and Co-Chair of the Great School Libraries campaign

When I started as a school librarian, this is exactly the book I needed. Now that it has been published, I have learned so much from it: new ideas and ways of working that I hadn't thought about before, which have prompted me to reflect on my own practice and think about areas I could improve.

One of the most exciting things about being a school librarian is the ability to develop our own library service and practice in the best way for our students and the school community. Many of us work on our own, or as part of a small team, and sometimes we don't seem to 'fit', being neither administrative nor teachers. But that is one of the strengths of our role – we support teaching and learning and we can also provide a safe and welcoming environment for the whole school community. We are on the frontline, finding the right book or the right information for the reader at the right time. As well as developing reading for pleasure, we can manage and develop our collection by identifying gaps and shortfalls in our stock and predicting new trends. Through supporting students with research, we can develop their information literacy and digital skills and help equip students for life beyond the classroom. In doing this, perhaps without realising it, we are also involved in all aspects of the profession of librarianship.

In joining the committee of the SLG, I have had the pleasure of working alongside some truly great and inspirational school librarians who have come together to write this book. I am sure that through sharing their wisdom they will inspire you and give you the confidence to grow and develop your own practice. My own small piece of advice is to make sure you get involved in the wider school library community, no matter how difficult it is to get the time or the money for your professional development. There is a huge network of school librarians and what has struck me most is how generous they are with their time and support and their willingness to give something back to the profession that we love.

Nick Cavender, BA PGDip, Vice Chair CILIP SLG

Abbreviations

ADHD	Attention Deficit Hyperactivity Disorder
ALA	American Library Association
ASCEL	Association of Senior Children's and Education Librarians
ASD	Autism Spectrum Disorder
CD	Conduct Disorder
CILIP	Chartered Institute of Library and Information Professionals (England, Wales and Northern Ireland)
CILIPS	Chartered Institute of Library and Information Professionals in Scotland
CRAAP	Currency, Relevance, Authority, Accuracy and Purpose
DDC	Dewey Decimal Classification
DfE	Department for Education (UK)
DLTF	Digital Literacy Task Force
EAL	English as an Additional Language
E-Portal	Another term for intranet
EPQ	Extended Project Qualification
EYFS	Early Years and Foundation Stage (Birth to 5 years) (England and Wales)
FE	Further Education
FSM	Free School Meals
GDPR	General Data Protection Regulation (UK)
GSL	Great School Libraries (Campaign)
HoD	Head of Department
HoY	Head of Year
IB	International Baccalaureate
IFLA	International Federation of Library Associations
IL	Information Literacy
ILG	CILIP Information Literacy Group
INSET	In-service Training

ISBN	International Standard Book Number
IT	Information Technology
JISC	Joint Information Systems Committee
LDP	Library Development Plan
LGBTQ+	Lesbian, Gay, Bisexual, Transgender, Queer or Questioning
LIPSSEE	Librarians in Independent Prep Schools in the South East of England
LMS	Library Management System
NC	National Curriculum (England)
NHS	National Health Service
NLT	National Literacy Trust
ODD	Oppositional Defiant Disorder
Ofsted	Office for Standards in Education, Children's Services and Skills
PDF	Portable Document Format
PLA	Pupil Library Assistant
PLAA	Pupil Library Assistant Award
PP	Pupil Premium
RADAR	Rationale, Authority, Date, Accuracy, Relevance
RfP	Reading for Pleasure
SDP	School Development Plan
SEN	Special Educational Needs
SENCo	Special Education Needs Co-ordinator
SEND	Special Educational Needs and Disabilities
SIFT	Stop, Investigate, Find, Trace
SIP	School Improvement Plan
SLA	School Library Association
SLG	CILIP School Libraries Group
SLIC	Scottish Library and Information Council
SLN	School Librarians Network
SLS	Schools Library Service
SLT	Senior (or School) Leadership Team
SMART targets	Specific, Measurable, Achievable, Realistic and Timely targets
SMT	Senior (or School) Management Team
SoW	Scheme of Work
SWOT	Strengths, Weaknesses, Opportunities and Threats
TA	Teaching Assistant
ToC	Theory of Change
UKLA	United Kingdom Literacy Association

UNESCO	United Nations Educational, Scientific and Cultural Organisation
YLG	CILIP Youth Libraries Group

Introduction

Ellen Krajewski

> It is an awfully sad misconception that librarians simply check books in and out.
> The library is the heart of a school, and without a librarian, it is but an empty
> shell.
> Jarret J. Krosoczka, www.brainyquote.com/quotes/jarrett_j_krosoczka_560729

These are challenging times for school librarians. This book has been developed by a group of experienced school library professionals to help and support newly appointed school librarians and those new to the information profession. At a time when school librarians can feel they are undervalued and under-appreciated there has never been a greater need for experienced professionals to share their knowledge and expertise with those at the beginning of their careers. Many schools are appointing someone with no library experience or qualifications to run their school library in the role of Librarian, Library Manager, Library Resource Centre (LRC) Manager, Library/LRC Co-ordinator or various other titles. For the purpose of this book, we will use the term 'school librarian' to refer to the person who has responsibility for running the school library.

The authors have all served on the SLG Committee and have 169 years of accumulated experience in school libraries between them. Caroline Roche has been Chair of CILIP's SLG for six years and this book was born out of her passion to ensure that every school has a trained librarian in post, in addition to a great school library. The individual chapters reflect areas of expertise and, as a whole, provide an indispensable aid to assist the newly appointed school librarian in navigating their way through the myriad of challenges they will face as they find the right path for developing their own school library.

The book reflects our position as librarians in England and uses terminology common in the UK, but we hope that the content will be equally relevant in other parts of the world.

At the time of writing, school libraries are not statutory in England, Wales and Northern Ireland and school librarians could be considered an endangered species. Yet school librarians use their knowledge and skills and, yes, their passion on a daily basis to inspire, encourage, empower and equip our young people with the skills they need to navigate the world of information. They teach research skills, evaluation and academic honesty. They introduce a wide variety of good quality and diverse literature to inspire and light the fires of imaginations. They fulfil a valuable pastoral role for those vulnerable or insecure students for whom the library is a safe haven.

School librarians continue their own learning through their ongoing professional development and then use that learning to help others. This book will help the new librarian discover how they too can take this journey, the key to job satisfaction and how to provide real impact on teaching, learning and extracurricular activities.

Many school librarians in England work alone with no other staff allocated to the library. However, some have a capable and enthusiastic team of student helpers and the Pupil Library Assistant of the Year Award (PLAA) acknowledges their contribution to a great school library. The Great School Libraries campaign (GSL) has been set up in a mission to bring libraries and access to librarians back to every school in the UK. The School Librarians Network (SLN) is an online forum, set up by Elizabeth Bentley, which provides the opportunity for school librarians to share ideas, discuss problems and challenges, build links and generally support each other. Add to these the various social media platforms of Facebook, Twitter, Pinterest and others, where school librarians can follow other librarians and educationalists, building up a professional network of contacts, and you begin to see the collaborative working that is part and parcel of being a school librarian. This book explores these connective pathways in depth and illustrates how they can be put into practice.

During 2020 and 2021, we faced a global pandemic. The rise and spread of COVID-19 resulted in a six-month lockdown closing schools and businesses. Online classrooms and home learning became the norm and school libraries faced a new challenge. Many school librarians were furloughed, leaving them unable to provide a library service at all. Others, working from home, rose to that challenge by putting in place online resources to support students, providing e-book platforms to encourage continued reading for pleasure and constantly searching for different ways to keep their library at the forefront of education. On the return to school, librarians operated within the COVID-19 and social distancing guidelines, bringing click and collect services to the school, online reviews and resources, including taking trolleys of books to other locations within the school to operate a mini-library.

The innovative and creative ways that school librarians continued to promote and provide their service were endless and, once again, highlighted the value and worth of a professional, qualified school librarian. When another two shorter lockdowns followed, the routines were already in place and school librarians rose up and met those challenges.

This book considers the use of virtual worlds and innovative technology and will help the new professional to deliver vital services in this way should there be demand. Maybe the era of a blended approach to learning is already upon us. No longer can school librarians just be perceived as curators of physical resources.

But every school library is different. What works like a dream in one will not work at all in another. School librarians have to be innovative, creative, reactive and very open-minded. They need to take ideas and adapt them to suit their own library environment. Some schools may be focused on raising literacy standards and developing a universal reading culture for their community, whereas other schools may concentrate on research skill competencies or the use of technology and virtual learning environments. Wherever we work, it is vital to keep up to date with the library and information world and also the education world.

This book offers a guide to the tools, skills and resources needed to become a successful school librarian. The individual chapters are succinct and allow you to explore the topics in the book as they become relevant to your situation. View the book as a starting block on which to build your career. We wish you every success in that venture!

The Role of the Library and Librarian within the School

Barbara Band

Introduction

The fundamental role of the school library and librarian is to support the mission and aims of the school, to support teaching and learning, and to provide for the needs of the school community. Some schools see the library's role as mainly supporting reading and, if this is the case, it is often under the remit of the English department and the librarian may have little contact with other departments. Other schools will view the library as a more academic space to be used for learning and quiet study, particularly by older students, and the librarian may find themselves in a more supervisory role.

Libraries operate within an environment that is constantly changing. Each year, a new cohort of students with varying needs arrives and older students leave; the curriculum changes, sometimes through legal requirements, at other times by staff choosing a different topic to study; there are educational initiatives announced by the government that require schools to change their priorities; and senior management set new targets and objectives for the school. In order to remain relevant, libraries must respond to all these changes.

The resources and services offered by the library can vary from school to school and will be impacted by how the school views its role. These may include:

- supporting learning to read, particularly in primary schools
- supporting initiatives to improve literacy levels
- promoting and supporting reading for pleasure
- providing a study space for students
- supporting teaching and learning in all curriculum areas

- delivering an information literacy programme
- providing a space that feeds into the wellbeing and mental health of students
- providing a range of extracurricular activities.

In an ideal world, every school library would be able to provide all these services. The reality is that many school librarians are solo workers with an endless to-do list, many only work term-time or part-time hours, and the management and administration of the library and its collection takes up a lot of time, making it difficult to consider a more strategic and long-term overview.

This chapter considers how the role of the library can support the school via its School Development Plan (SDP) and how this feeds into the Library Development Plan (LDP). The demographics and needs of the school community are used as a starting point for providing an inclusive range of resources and services. Legally required documents and how these impact on the library are discussed, as are useful library documents such as a school library policy and annual report. Finally, copyright and safeguarding with respect to school libraries are briefly covered.

School mission statement and School Development Plan

Every school will have a mission statement that outlines its values and objectives. This is usually found on the school website. A mission statement is a formal announcement of the aims of the school; it provides a brief overview of the school's ethos and defines its educational goals and purpose. It is a statement to parents/carers, staff and students about what the school wants to achieve.

For example:

> 'Our mission is to provide a high quality education in a respectable and inclusive environment that enables every student to reach their full potential,' or 'Our school empowers all students to embrace learning, achieve their personal best and build their emotional, social and physical wellbeing.'
>
> Drew, 2021

An SDP – sometimes known as the School Improvement Plan (SIP) – is a strategic document used for raising standards and, together with any recommendations from the latest Ofsted (or other inspection) report, will determine actions needed by individuals and departments to improve the school's goals. The SDP is usually long-term, covering a period of approximately three to five years. Although it will draw on internal data, it can only be written after the school has evaluated its performance so is usually revisited in the summer, after exam results are published, in order for priorities to be reassessed.

An SDP is not a list of what the school will do; it is a list of key objectives and targets needed to increase performance. These must be SMART (specific, measurable, achievable, realistic and timely), have success criteria, which are both quantitative and qualitative, and indicate resource requirements and responsibilities.

However, targets will not remain static and can change depending on any future inspection reports, test and exam results or education initiatives. For example, if test results show falling literacy levels within a year group, increasing these may become a school priority. Likewise, if statistics indicate that few students move on to higher education, the school may decide to focus on projects that raise students' aspirations and career progression. For an example, see Table 1.1 below.

Table 1.1 *Example School Development Plan – Equality and Diversity Action Plan*

Target	Audit whole school curriculum to ensure it is promoting positive images of ethnic minorities
Impact	Ethnic minority students develop a positive self-image Curriculum reflects multicultural society Stereotypes are challenged and mindsets changed Create more outward-looking and tolerant school community
Strategies	Senior Management Team (SMT) to audit all Schemes of Work (SoW) Subject leaders to ensure the curriculum promotes current issues Teachers to ensure resources and displays reflect ethnic minorities
Timescale	Ongoing
Resources	Staff time Learning resources

School management use the SDP to ascertain school priorities and allocate funding. Before you plan any library priorities and activities it is, therefore, important to obtain the SDP and any inspection reports so that you are aware of the overall objectives of the school.

Library Development Plan

It can be useful for the library to have a mission statement. This will determine its ethos and enable you to state its purpose to the wider community, highlighting what the library does and why. The statement should be on the school website and displayed in the library. For example: 'The mission of the school library is to provide materials and services to help students obtain information to meet their personal, educational and cultural needs', or 'The mission of the school library is to ensure that students are effective and ethical users of information and technology, empowering them to be critical thinkers and lifelong learners'.

The next step is to create an LDP that links with the SDP and any inspection recommendations. The plan will show how the library supports the actions in these documents. It should be written using the same format and headings, with outcomes, a timeframe, resource requirements, budget needs and training requirements. An LDP can help determine priorities, guide and motivate staff, assist with time management and allocate funding. Although it should be long-term, in reality most LDPs cover a period of one or two years. Since library budgets are awarded annually, the LDP has to be assessed in line with any new funding.

The LDP will be based on knowledge of the community and their needs and expectations, together with the current status of the library collection. It provides measures of accountability and success to senior management and governors. The LDP should also link with curriculum areas.

Support from senior management is essential, so discuss how the library can support the SDP with your line manager and other relevant staff before writing it and assigning objectives and targets. This also helps develop ownership and support of the library.

For example, if an SDP target is to raise the literacy level of Key Stage 3 (KS3) boys, the LDP could include:

- undertaking a student survey to ascertain reading and leisure interests
- carrying out a stock audit to determine what current resources meet the needs highlighted by the survey, sourcing additional resource requirements and purchasing them – this will have staff time and funding implications.
- promoting the new resources via the library management system (LMS), displays and book talks in assemblies
- organising various activities to engage KS3 boys with reading, including author visits, book talks in library lessons, running reading groups and competitions
- collecting loan statistics and other data, such as engagement with activities, as well as anecdotal comments from students and staff, to determine outcomes
- publishing details of the impact of your initiatives in a brief report sent to the SMT.

In the example of the SDP given in Table 1.1 on p. 3, it is easy to see how the school library could support this by providing details of diverse and inclusive resources that could be used within the curriculum, website addresses of organisations that provide relevant display materials, creating multicultural library lists and displays that link with curriculum areas, etc. However, not all SDP actions translate so easily into library actions and may need further discussion with your line manager or those responsible for its implementation to determine whether the library can have a useful input.

Supporting the school community

A school community consists of several stakeholders with varying needs: students, staff, senior management, governors and parents/carers. All these needs should be taken into account when you are developing the library collection, creating services and providing information.

It can be useful to undertake a needs audit of the school community to use as a starting point when planning the purchase of resources and organising events and activities. This information can also be used as a benchmark when carrying out a diversity audit of the collection. The needs of the school community will certainly influence collection management, including their classification, catalogue keywording and labelling.

Some information can be obtained from outside sources. The Office for National Statistics (www.ons.gov.uk/peoplepopulationandcommunity) has a wide range of information on cultural identities, household characteristics and population demographics, as well as a guide for where to look for local statistics. This information will give you an idea about the features of the local community that feed into the school population.

Within the school, the admissions officer will be able to tell you how many students are from minority ethnic backgrounds and what their cultural heritage is, how many are EAL (English as an Additional Language) students and what other languages are spoken, what faiths are represented and how many pupil premium students you have. The more information you can gather about your student population, the better you will be able to provide relevant resources for them.

The pastoral team will be able to provide information on those who have family issues, students who have experienced bereavement or are coping with terminal illness within the family, and any who are questioning their gender identity. The Special Educational Needs Co-ordinator (SENCo) will be able to give you information on neurodiverse students and those who have other learning or behavioural difficulties.

Sometimes you can meet resistance when asking for this information, so it is important to explain that you need it in order to provide appropriate resources for all students, not just those who visit the library and whose needs you are aware of.

Students

This group will have varying needs as a result of the range of ages, abilities, cultures and interests. At primary level they will require support with learning to read; at secondary level the school may well run a reading scheme that involves the library. Students with learning difficulties will have different needs, such as books printed on a different coloured background. Book selection should take into account the reading levels of students – discussion with the English department, as well as the SENCo, will help determine these.

In addition to supporting learning to read, the library plays a role in reading for pleasure, reading to support the curriculum and reading for leisure interests. The demographics of the school community, obtained through a needs audit, will help you to select resources that reflect the students' lives and backgrounds. It is important that the whole school community see themselves represented within the library: in characters and illustrations; in writers and illustrators; and in displays and promotions. The ethnicity, culture and faith within the school should be represented within the collection by books on different countries, festivals and celebrations, food and traditional tales. There should be bilingual books for all EAL students. Having a wide-ranging and diverse collection will help you support diversity throughout the curriculum.

Information about students' reading and interests can be obtained via surveys and informal discussions with them. Some interests remain constant – for example, football, cars, dinosaurs and pets. Others vary from school to school or are impacted by recent trends and national events. For example, the Rugby World Cup tends to generate an interest in the sport and this can be used to great effect in a display featuring linked fiction and non-fiction books. Find out what books and authors students have enjoyed reading, as well as any books they may have read at previous schools, and use this information to promote similar genres or books by the same authors. Although most librarians survey Year 7 students, it can be useful to carry out regular surveys amongst older students as their interests – and thus needs – will have changed. The exercise will also act as a reminder that the library has resources of use to them.

The pastoral needs of students should not be ignored. Students will require information on personal development, general health and life skills, as well as resources to support their mental health and wellbeing, such as books about bullying, bereavement and dealing with stress.

Staff

The focus of the teaching staff will be on delivering the National Curriculum and meeting both departmental and SDP targets. At primary level, all staff will be involved in teaching reading; at secondary level this is often left to the English department although if a school has developed a whole school reading ethos then reading will have a wider staff remit. Staff who are involved in reading will want to know how the library can support them and are likely to want information about new resources, suggested book lists, details about activities, etc., that they can use with their students.

Teaching staff will be interested in resources that support their teaching and learning, such as books and material they can direct students to which extend their reading within subjects and that help with any homework or projects. Other useful information includes relevant websites and online resources. As well as providing subject resources, the library is also a learning space where the librarian can help students find resources and information for both personal and academic needs. This may be on an ad-hoc basis or via research lessons. Some librarians are involved in delivering an information literacy skills programme.

The school website, exam board websites and SoW for each department will help you identify curriculum topics but not all of these will have a resource need. Some may simply be delivered during one lesson with no linked homework, whilst others could be studied over several lessons and include homework assignments or projects.

Other staff within the school that the librarian will work with, and whose needs should be considered, include: teaching assistants, the SENCo and the pastoral team, who will be working with individual students; those responsible for marketing/social media, who will be interested in anything they can promote to parents, such as competitions and author visits; the literacy co-ordinator, who is responsible for literacy initiatives throughout the school; and the careers administrator.

Collaboration and communication with teaching staff will help to identify where the library can be of most use, so it is important for the librarian to attend departmental meetings. While it is possible to send an email to all staff asking for their resource requirements, this is likely to be ignored in a busy school. It is easier to determine their needs by having a quick conversation with them. This can be done when they are in the library or you meet them in the staff room, but be aware that they are likely to be concentrating on their class or looking forward to a short break. It is better if you can arrange to meet them at a mutually convenient time. Create a grid for all subjects and year groups and use it to fill in the required information. Specific information is more useful than a broad general topic – see Table 1.2 below.

Table 1.2 *Using a grid to support curriculum topics*

Geography	Autumn term 1	Autumn term 2
Year 7	Basic map skills Local land use	Identifying landforms Major world mountains and rivers
Year 8	Earthquakes and volcanoes Charities and disaster responses	Formation and identification of rocks Erosion

Senior management and governors

This group makes decisions about the school, allocates budgets and determines its priorities. They will want to know what value and benefits the library brings to the school, as well as how it supports the SDP. They require brief reports detailing both quantitative and qualitative data around budgets, library use and impact. Be aware that some senior management staff will also have teaching responsibilities and, therefore, have the same needs as other teaching staff.

Parents and carers

This group is interested in how they can support their children with learning at home, as well as how the school is supporting them during the school day. They need to be kept informed of events and activities within the library and provided with book lists to support their child's reading. It is important to engage with parents as they can be supportive of the school library. There are several ways to connect with parents/carers: ensure that any information about the library on the school website is up to date; send out regular library newsletters (either hard copy or digital) and/or include library news on school newsletters; provide suggested reading lists for year groups, as well as for less-able and more-able readers; and promote any internal and external reading-related events and activities, such as competitions and author interviews.

School and legal documentation

In addition to the SDP and inspection report, there are a range of other documents and legal requirements that impact on the library, its collection and services. These include, but are not limited to:

■ The Equality Act 2010 (www.legislation.gov.uk/ukpga/2010/15) lists nine protected characteristics and protects against discrimination or unfair treatment. In schools, this means students cannot be discriminated against because of their sex, race, disability, religion or belief, or sexual orientation. For the library, this means ensuring you have a wide range of diverse resources and that any displays and promotional events are also inclusive.

■ The Data Protection Act (DPA) 2018 (www.legislation.gov.uk/ukpga/2018/12) controls how your personal information is used. Everyone responsible for using personal data has to follow its principles. There is stronger protection for sensitive information such as ethnic background, religious beliefs and biometrics. Under the Act, a person has a right to know what information is stored about them and how it is used. Data must only be used for specified purposes, it must be accurate and up to date, and must be held securely. It should also not be held for longer than is needed. It is important to note that personal data belongs to the student – a parent/carer can only access it if the student is unable to act on their own behalf. Schools usually include privacy notices when data is first collected that detail how and why data will be used or shared.

■ The UK General Data Protection Regulation (GDPR) came into force in May 2018 and deals with the collection and handling of data, including how to respond to security breaches. The DPA is the implementation of the GDPR. For school libraries, the DPA will cover details of students' borrowing records, as well as taking photos or videos of them. If the library uses a biometric fingerprint recognition system, this is also covered by the Act and the government has published advice regarding the protection of biometric data (DfE, 2018). Biometric data cannot be collected without parental consent and, even with parental consent, the student can refuse to provide it. Once a student has left the school, all data relating to them should be deleted from the LMS. The school should have a designated Data Protection Officer who can advise you if necessary.

As well as the above statutory policies required by UK law, there are a range of education-related policies that all schools should have, including: a behaviour management and discipline policy; an anti-bullying policy; an equity and diversity policy; a health and safety policy; a safeguarding policy; a teaching and learning policy; a literacy strategy; and an IT policy. The librarian needs to be aware of all of these and how they can influence the library with regards to collection development and management, services offered and library use. It is important for the librarian to know the discipline procedures and rewards/sanctions system used within the school and to have the authority to implement this in the library. IT policies are also very relevant, particularly if the library has any IT equipment, as they cover its use, including accessing websites and social media.

School library policy

A school library policy is a framework for the operation of the library that enables it to be managed effectively and efficiently. It explains the purpose and function of the library, as well as the main services and practices offered by the librarian to the school community. It can be used to provide consistent standards and is a means of communication and advocacy. The policy should meet any legal requirements, be applied without discrimination and should consist of broad statements that cover:

- the management and use of the library, such as the booking system, expected behaviour required of students, any ad hoc use and opening hours
- the staffing of the library – hours worked and by whom, formal arrangements for meetings with other staff, INSET training, outside meetings with other school library groups
- the responsibilities of library staff
- how the library supports and encourages reading, including library lessons, events and activities
- the physical facilities provided by the library, including soft seating, tables and chairs for study, IT provision
- details regarding the stock collection, including the purchase, classification and arrangement of resources, as well as how donations are treated
- other library services provided, such as information literacy skills lessons, support for students undertaking Extended Project Qualifications (EPQ).

The policy needs to be succinct; if it is too long it is unlikely to be read. It should be written using the same format and template as other school policies, using education rather than library terminology – do not assume that readers know what the Dewey Decimal System or keywords are – and sent to your line manager and SMT. A library policy should be reviewed regularly as school and government policies change over time. Remember, the library policy does not exist on its own but within the context of the policies, ethos and aims of the school. It can be useful to include stakeholders in the development of the library policy, perhaps in the form of a library steering group or working party. This can contain students, other staff, governors or even parents; including others will ensure the policy is not insular and gives stakeholders ownership of, and involvement in, the library.

Detailed procedures and rules should be in a library handbook rather than in the policy statement. The handbook expands on the policy and contains the actions to be taken in particular circumstances. For example, the school library policy will make reference to the Equality Act 2010 and the school's Equality and Diversity policy with regards to the purchasing of new resources. It will contain a brief statement about the classification and labelling of all resources – fiction and non-fiction. The library handbook will have a lot more detail about the classification systems used, such as whether fiction is labelled and shelved according to the author's surname; the size and colour of the labels used; the size and colour of the font if printed; whether one or two alphabetical letters are used; whether fiction resources are labelled with reading levels; and whether there is one long run of fiction or it is divided into quick read, a main collection and senior fiction, etc. These details will provide a useful guide for new staff or any volunteers within the library and will ensure continuity with regards to library processes.

Annual report

Another important document that needs to be produced is the annual report. This provides an overview of library activities during the previous year; it may or may not be written at the same time as the budget review. An annual report tends to be produced at the end of the school year in July; budget reports are likely to follow the financial year used within the school.

The annual report will give an overview of the library and a snapshot of the collection and its usage, but its main focus should be the impact the library has had, the difference you have made and how you have supported both the SDP and teaching and learning within the school. It can be useful to include the LDP, as well as collection and usage statistics. Use your LMS to obtain this information along with data on reading and literacy; many have pre-set reports in their programmes that can be adapted for individual libraries.

Remember, the library is competing against other departments, so you need to demonstrate value for money, as well as highlighting any achievements. By linking the LDP to the SDP and then analysing actions on the LDP, you can show how you have helped the school reach its targets and goals. One way to demonstrate impact is via quantitative data, such as book loans, footfall and participation statistics, particularly if these are linked to a specific activity, but providing qualitative data will have more influence. Statements can be collected from students and staff, as well as evidence that the library has affected behaviour in the classroom.

For example, if you are delivering an information literacy skills programme you could ask teachers if they have noticed students using a wider range of resources for their research and whether these have been evaluated to ensure they are accurate and relevant or, if you are giving book talks, whether these have increased the range of authors and genres read by the students.

When writing the report, think about the intended audience and their information needs. Identify essentials such as the main purpose of the report and what actions you want people to take; these can be listed as recommendations or conclusions. The language you use should be positive – use words such as opportunity, contribution and successful – and present evidence in a visually appealing way using charts and infographics as this has more immediate impact.

The report can be sent to your Headteacher, line manager, bursar and link governor (or chair of governors if you do not have one). Remember, as well as being a document that demonstrates how the library, and thus you, support the school, it is also a tool for advocacy and promotion.

You may like to consider producing informal termly reports to send to your line manager. These can then be used to create your annual report, provide a starting point for discussion during any meetings and have the added bonus of ensuring your line manager is aware of what you are doing to support the school community.

If you are also producing a financial report, this should detail all funding received and how it was spent against the financial plan and LDP. It will show where costs were higher than anticipated and if there were any overspends, why and on what. The annual report and financial plan can be used to support future funding bids.

Copyright

Copyright is an area that creates a lot of confusion within schools with even teaching staff unaware of what they are legally entitled to do. As the school librarian, you are in a unique position to advise staff of legal requirements with regards to the use of other materials and resources. As well as informing staff, it is important to ensure that students know about copyright, the use of referencing and acknowledging sources in their work.

It is understandable that people want to try and obtain resources for as little cost as possible. However, no one would dream of going into a bookshop and taking a few books because 'the school can't afford to buy them' and yet it is sometimes considered acceptable to use illegally downloaded PDFs of the same book. Schools do have some leeway regarding copyright; they are entitled to copy up to 5% of a book and make multiple copies of those pages for educational purposes. What they cannot do is copy 5% each time until they have copied the whole book.

For further information, the website Copyright and Schools (copyrightandschools.org) covers the different licences required for different activities in schools throughout the UK. It has information about centralised agreements for schools and includes written works, TV and radio, film, music, and online and digital resources. It is an easy way to check what the school may need for sharing, copying or using materials.

Safeguarding

Schools have a statutory requirement with regards to safeguarding the welfare of students and all staff are legally required to undertake safeguarding training. This includes staff in maintained as well as independent schools and academies, including further education and sixth form colleges.

Safeguarding and the welfare of students is everyone's responsibility and all staff are involved in creating a safe environment in which students can learn. The librarian has an important role to play in this aspect as they are in a position to identify concerns, provide resources and pass on anything that they feel needs further investigation. The library is often a 'safe' space within the school, somewhere a student can go at breaktimes if they are being bullied, if they have not yet found their 'place' within their peer group or if they feel overwhelmed by the busyness of the rest of the school. Librarians see many students on a regular basis, often every day, so may be able to identify any changes in behaviour. Breaktimes allow students to have a more informal chat with the librarian, which may help to identify any issues.

There are certain school documents that the librarian should be aware of with respect to safeguarding. These include the child protection policy, behaviour policy and staff behaviour policy (or code of conduct). Schools will also have a designated safeguarding lead who is usually a member of the SMT.

The librarian should be aware of what to do if they are concerned about a student and who to approach to voice their concerns. Safeguarding requires a holistic approach involving all staff who may have contact with the student; this includes the librarian so it is important you are aware of any issues that may impact on their wellbeing, mental health and behaviour. For further information please see the DfE document *Keeping Children Safe in Education* (2021a).

Action points

1 Analyse the SDP with regards to how the library can support its targets and objectives.
2 Obtain departmental SoW and highlight areas where the library may be able to provide resources and support.
3 Consider the needs of the student body – how would you find these out?
4 Do your existing resources and services provide for all needs?
5 Are you aware of the school policies? These should be accessible on the school website. Read them and consider how they impact on library provision.

Further reading

American Association of School Libraries (2018) *Position Statement on the Definition of an Effective School Library*, www.ala.org/aasl/sites/ala.org.aasl/files/content/advocacy/statements/docs/AASL_Position_Statement_Effective_SLP_2018.pdf.

Australian Library and Information Association School & Victorian Catholic Teacher Librarians (2017) *A Manual for Developing Policies and Procedures in Australian School Library Resource Centres*, 2nd edn, ALIA, https://read.alia.org.au/manual-developing-policies-and-procedures-australian-school-library-resource-centres-2nd-edition.

Clark, C. and Teravainen, A. (2017) *School Libraries: A Literature Review of Current Provision and Evidence of Impact*, National Literacy Trust, https://cdn.literacytrust.org.uk/media/documents/2017_06_30_free_research_-_school_library_review_XxR5qcv.pdf.

Merga, M., Roni, S., Chin, E. and Malpique, A. (2021) Revisiting Collaboration Within and Beyond the School Library: New Ways of Measuring Effectiveness, *Journal of Library Administration*, **61** (3), 332–346, www.tandfonline.com/doi/full/10.1080/01930826.2021.1883370?src.

NHS Health Education England and Brettle, A. (n.d.) *Value and Impact Toolkit*, with details about various tools that can be used for measuring services, https://kfh.libraryservices.nhs.uk/value-and-impact-toolkit.

Scholastic (2016) *School Libraries Work! A Compendium of Research Supporting the Effectiveness of School Libraries*, www.scholastic.com/SLW2016/index.html.

Scottish Library and Information Council (n.d.) *How Good is Our School Library?* https://scottishlibraries.org/advice-guidance/frameworks/how-good-is-our-school-library.

2

The Library Environment

Barbara Band

Introduction

A library does not stand alone within a school. Its character is determined by the support it receives and how libraries are viewed by the school community. It can be a buzzy exciting place that is at the centre of the school or a rarely-used room stuck in an outbuilding. The library environment includes several features: the physical space; the resources held within it; the visual aspects; the staff; and the character created by all of these. A school library is greater than the sum of its parts and therefore all its features need to be considered.

The physical space

School libraries vary considerably in size. Those in primary schools tend to be smaller and are often found along a corridor, situated in an open space within the building such as the reception area, or even housed in a portacabin or decommissioned bus in the playground. Secondary school libraries, generally, are located within a purpose-built room, large enough to accommodate several students as well as an extensive resource collection. However, this is not always the case: some primary schools have purpose-built libraries whilst some secondary schools have libraries squeezed into small rooms. Nevertheless, the Great School Libraries survey reported that 'the nature and use of school library spaces varies significantly, with primary schools less likely than secondary schools to have a dedicated library space (as opposed to an open plan/multi-purpose space)' (2019).

There are several factors to consider with regards to the physical library:

- As a whole school resource, it should be centrally located, accessible and welcoming to all members of the school community. If it is tucked away in a corner of the school or up a flight of stairs, it is unlikely to get 'passing traffic' – an ideal location would be near the reception or dining area, somewhere that students visit regularly or pass by during the course of their day. Accessibility for disabled students and staff also needs to be considered.
- It should have sufficient lighting, preferably natural, and adequate ventilation and heating. Working in a dim, stuffy room is depressing for both students and staff and can make concentration difficult. Low lighting may also cause issues for students with visual disabilities, but if the lights are too bright, they can cause glare and reflections on screens.
- There are no recommended guidelines for how many students the library should be able to accommodate but, at the very least, it should be large enough to seat one whole class, preferably at tables. If the library is only large enough to allow use by a handful of students at a time, then library and research lessons cannot take place.
- The space should also be flexible enough to allow a variety of activities including independent study, group work and leisure reading. Ideally, it should be able to accommodate a whole class in addition to ad hoc visits from students carrying out research tasks, as well as older students undertaking independent study.
- The library furniture should include soft seating, tables and chairs as well as a range of shelving and display units suitable for a collection of varied resources, including fiction, non-fiction, graphic novels, magazines, audio books and more. The organisation of these resources should be obvious to all users.
- The school library should provide relevant access to information technology in the form of computers and/or mobile devices, as well as digital resources. A library management system (LMS) is essential for efficient and effective management of the library.
- The library should have an issue desk sited to facilitate supervision of the space, as well as secure office space and storage.

Library layout

The layout of the library will be determined by the size and shape of the available space. However, there are aspects relevant to all libraries regardless of their size. The issue desk should be near the entrance so students are immediately aware of where they can go to ask for help. It should be placed so that there are clear sight lines along all the shelving and to facilitate supervision of any students working in the library.

Although it may not be possible to cater for the needs of all students at the same time, the space should allow for various activities, including quiet reading on soft seating, individual independent study, whole-class lessons at tables, group work and after-school activities. Additionally, it can be useful to have the space to hold larger meetings, such as the student council or LGBTQ+ group, with furniture that can be arranged as per a conference or theatre layout. Shelving needs to be far enough apart to allow for browsing and there should be enough space around displays for students to peruse the resources and information.

It should be noted that secondary schools will usually have far more meetings and activities happening in the library, so the furniture and space requirements are likely to be different from those of primary school libraries.

Library furniture

Library furniture and fittings are expensive, so it is important that any purchases are fit for purpose. Although it is possible to buy cheaper shelving from high street stores, it is unlikely to be able to cope with the demands of a busy library and will soon show signs of wear and tear. It is also more likely to break or warp under the weight of books. The library may already have shelving fitted but if you are in the position of refurbishing or creating a new library, there are companies who offer a planning service, as well as supplying suitable furniture, such as Gresswell (www.gresswell.co.uk), FG Library and Learning (www.fglibrary.co.uk) and Peters (www.peters.co.uk). Some school library consultants also offer this service.

It is important to consider the intended use of the library before planning the layout, as well as investigating library designs. There are several examples online via sites such as Pinterest and Instagram and it could be useful to visit local schools with refurbished libraries to gather recommendations and advice. Some library furniture is quite unusual and has a 'wow' factor but, in use, is not particularly practical. A bookcase shaped like a tree with randomly placed shelves representing branches may look attractive but is restrictive with regards to the books that can be placed on it and keeping them in any sort of order would be very difficult.

Shelving needs to be a suitable height for students. Primary school libraries should have lower shelving than that found in secondary school libraries – if shelving is too high, younger students cannot reach the resources, plus it is unlikely to meet disability requirements. The shelving also needs to be appropriate for different sizes of books; normally, fiction books are smaller in height than non-fiction resources, which will need more space between individual shelves.

Consideration should be given to the storage of picture books and graphic novels, as well as other resources, such as audio books. Primary school libraries are likely to have more picture books for under 8-year-olds, although secondary school libraries could have 'picture books for older readers' and if the library interacts with local primary schools or runs sessions involving parents and younger children, they may want to have a selection of picture books as well. These books are best stored in kinderboxes or on shelving units designed for picture books to facilitate browsing.

The library shelving should allow for books to be shown face out to attract students. The library should also incorporate display areas so that particular aspects of the stock can be promoted or linked with school and national events. For example, displays promoting national book awards or books related to Black History Month or World Environment Day can introduce students to areas of the collection they may not be aware of.

Stock classification

Classification of the stock is necessary for the effective use of the library. It allows for resources to be organised, facilitates searching for specific authors and subjects, and makes it easier to find items on the shelves. Resources are usually divided into fiction and non-fiction and each will be classified differently.

Traditionally, fiction is classified using the author's last name and shelved in alphabetical order from A to Z. Sometimes one letter is used; at other times two or three letters. In primary schools, phonics is taught using reading schemes with books levelled into bands represented by colours; occasionally the librarian is asked to classify the school library's early years resources to fit into this scheme but generally an alphabetical sequence will be used. It is possible to classify fiction books by genre using alphabetical order within each category. This, however, may separate books written by the same author; for example, Malorie Blackman has written books that could be considered science fiction/dystopian as well as crime/adventure stories and in a genre classified library these would not be in the same sections. It is also necessary to know the main genre of each book before it can be classified and there is the problem of what to do with books that do not seem to easily fit into one specific genre.

Although there are many classification systems, non-fiction resources in schools are frequently classified using the Dewey Decimal Classification (DDC) system. This divides all non-fiction books into ten categories from 000–

999, with decimal points added for further breakdowns of topics within a subject. The ten main divisions are:

000 Computer science, information and general reference
100 Philosophy and psychology
200 Religion
300 Society/social sciences
400 Language
500 Science
600 Technology (applied science)
700 Arts and recreation
800 Literature
900 History, biography and geography

An example of a further breakdown within a main Dewey division could be:

300 – Society/social sciences
370 – Education
373 – Secondary education
373.25 – Comprehensive schools

A simplified DDC system tends to be employed within school libraries, usually with minimal decimal points. Some schools may also use coloured labels to identify the major ten DDC categories or shelve non-fiction books according to curriculum topics. This is often the case within primary school libraries. However, using both coloured labels and simplified DDC numbers enables younger students to identify subject areas by colour and older students to learn how to use the DDC system, which they are likely to experience at secondary school and in the majority of public libraries.

Using an established system facilitates the transfer of library skills between school stages, as well as into further and higher education. The key to any classification system is consistency and it is best to decide what to use prior to cataloguing resources. Online sources, such as the Online Computer Library Centre (OCLC), a global library co-operative (www.oclc.org/en/dewey.html) and the British Library (http://explore.bl.uk), can be used to help with the selection of Dewey numbers.

Cataloguing resources

Most school libraries will operate using a computerised library management system (LMS), a relational database that keeps an inventory of all catalogued stock and records the borrowing of resources, linking various sets of data. Cataloguing library stock enables students and staff to search the collection for relevant resources and find them in the library as each resource is listed with basic bibliographic data, such as title, author, publisher and date of publication, as well as its classification details. Many LMSs allow additional information to be recorded, such as genres, subjects and keywords; these allow for detailed searches to be carried out, enabling students and staff to find resources linked to their interests or the curriculum.

As with classifying resources, consistency is key when cataloguing stock. It can be useful to create a cataloguing policy with guidelines detailing the stages that need to be completed and required information to be inputted; otherwise, the catalogue is likely to contain anomalies and errors. For example, when cataloguing series, decide whether the order should be series name then title or title first then series name. When resources are catalogued, each will be given a unique barcode so that multiple copies of the same book can be identified. The spine is then labelled according to the classification system used, whether this is letters, coloured labels and/or Dewey numbers.

Labels should be clear and uncluttered to aid students with learning difficulties or visual disabilities. To facilitate access to resources, there should be shelf guiding and a subject index; in primary schools this is usually a wall chart, with a detailed alphabetical subject guide provided in secondary schools. These can be purchased from companies such as Carel Press (https://carelpress.uk) who will supply the information in a spreadsheet file that can be amended to suit individual circumstances. Schools Library Services also often have subject indexes available for subscribers or at a cost.

Library management systems

There are several LMSs available. Free LMSs are very basic and usually restrict the number and type of resources that can be included. Other LMSs offer a range of facilities, including detailed records with additional bibliographic information, report writing, bespoke lists and automatic overdue reminders. LMSs enable the library to be managed efficiently and save time. They can also be used to promote the library to students and staff outside the library space as they can be accessed remotely. This enables students to check their loans, search the catalogue and reserve books. In addition, the librarian can promote new stock and highlight any library news or activities.

When deciding on an LMS for the school library, it is important to consider the requirements of the library and ensure that what is purchased can meet these. LMS companies offer demonstrations – it can also be useful to visit local schools that are operating the system to see it in action. There are several factors that need to be considered:

■ The more features an LMS has, the more expensive it is likely to be. There will also be other costs associated with installation, such as integration with the school management system.
■ Annual subscription fees that cover upgrades and ongoing support will need to be paid.
■ The existing library hardware has to be capable of supporting the system. If it does not, it may need to be upgraded.
■ If training is required, ascertain if this will be provided free-of-charge or if there is an additional cost.

The main LMS systems include: Accessit (https://accessitlibrary.com); Heritage Cirqa (https://isoxford.com); Libresoft (http://libresoft.co.uk); Oliver (www.softlinkint.com); Pergamon Mu (www.esferico.net); and Reading Cloud (www.readingcloud.net).

Technology in the library

In addition to the LMS, there may be other technology found within the library. This is more likely to be the case with secondary school libraries rather than primary school libraries due to costs and available space, as well as each having a different focus and use within the school. Technology enhances library provision, allowing students to explore, create and learn. It also helps students to become digitally literate, an important and necessary skill in the 21st century (see Chapter 5: Information and Digital Literacy for further information). If the library is going to incorporate digital resources as part of the collection, it is necessary to have the technology that allows the access and use of them both within and outside the library.

Technology that may be found in libraries includes:

■ PCs, laptops or tablets: some secondary schools have an IT suite off the library or enough PCs or laptops stored in a trolley for a whole class to use. However, if the library is used as a classroom with students using the IT facilities but not the resources, it can prevent access by other students during those times. Ideally, the use of technology should be an integrated part of a library lesson rather than the only reason for booking the space
■ e-readers that can be used to engage students who struggle with or dislike reading, as well as aiding those with visual disabilities

- an interactive smartboard for use during lessons and that can be used to show presentations and videos
- equipment that allows the use of augmented and virtual reality.

There are various aspects to consider with regards to technology within the library. The initial costs can be quite high, although these should come out of an IT budget rather than the library budget. Any equipment will need to be maintained and updated, otherwise new software and applications may not be supported, and there may be subscription costs involved. It is also important that the school's WiFi is adequate to allow the use of technology within the library (see Chapter 6: Using Technology to Enhance the Library Experience for further information).

Library staff

In the UK, the situation with regards to staff in the school library varies considerably, partly because there is no legal requirement to have a school library let alone a school librarian. The CILIP Guidelines for Secondary School Libraries (Shaper, 2014, 8) recommend that the librarian:

- is line managed by a senior management team (SMT) member with responsibility for curriculum development
- is consulted and included in improvement planning to influence the strategic direction of the school
- has direct access to the strategic management of the school, so that the library can play a full role in school improvement
- has Head of Department status so that the librarian can listen to, understand and meet the needs of all departments within the school and play a full and proactive part in improvement planning on a par with other Heads of Departments
- is responsible for feeding into the annual reporting process in line with academic departments
- is not associated with any one particular teaching department and works effectively across the curriculum
- has a relationship with the governing body in line with other Heads of Department
- is included in all staff appraisals and training and participates in the delivery of relevant staff INSET
- is salaried at a level commensurate with other Departmental Heads.

The reality is that school librarians are managed by a range of people including: Headteachers; a member of the SMT; the Head of English; an English teacher or teacher from another department; the literacy co-ordinator; and the finance manager or bursar. Ideally, school librarians should be managed by a person with an overview of the curriculum and with the authority to support library initiatives; being managed by a member of the English team may result in the library being seen as an extension of the English department rather than a whole school resource.

A job description will outline the main tasks and responsibilities of the role; they can be generic or very detailed. The person specification for the position details the essential and desirable qualities required. It should be noted that in many schools the 'librarian' is given an alternative title such as the 'learning resource centre manager' or the 'reading ambassador', but usually the job description is one that you would expect to see for a librarian. Likewise, the 'library' is often called the 'learning resource centre' or 'media resource centre'. It is interesting to note that, despite what the librarian and library are called, students, staff and parents still tend to use the recognised terms of 'librarian' and 'library'.

Traditionally, there is a hierarchical staff structure ranging from the Head Librarian through to assistant librarians and library assistants. However, as many school librarians are solo workers, they are often responsible for the management of the school library and so are the 'librarian' regardless of what they are called. In primary schools, it is usual for the librarian to either be a part-time worker or have an additional role, such as a teaching assistant.

Volunteers, both adults and students, can play an important role in the school library, particularly if the librarian is a solo worker. Volunteers can take on administrative work, help with re-shelving books, tidying the stock and putting up displays, thus freeing up the librarian to focus on more strategic plans. They can also assist with library events and activities. Many schools use student volunteers; in primary schools these are often from Year 6, whilst in secondary schools it is more usual to use Key Stage 3 students (Years 7–9), although some schools use volunteers up to and including the sixth form. It is important that volunteers receive training and are made to feel they are part of the team so create a rota for them and ensure there is a range of tasks that use their skills and expertise, whether this is attention to detail in putting stock away or a creative flair in producing posters. Regular adult volunteers will need to undergo safeguarding training and have a Disclosure and Barring Service (DBS) check; ad hoc volunteers do not need to do this but must not be left alone with students.

With regards to student volunteers, it can be useful to instigate a training programme over a period of weeks that covers various aspects of the library, including operating the LMS at breaktimes. Being part of a student library team can help students develop useful workplace skills, such as collaboration and communication. It can also increase their self-confidence and give them a sense of ownership of the library. The School Library Association has a Pupil Librarian Toolkit (available to members) with a structured training programme and certificates at different levels.

The CILIP School Libraries Group and the School Library Association run a joint UK Pupil Library Assistant of the Year Award that is open to all student volunteers. Many Schools Library Services also run local awards. Entering student library assistants for these is an excellent way to showcase their contribution.

Library qualifications

Library qualifications include both academic and professional. Library and information studies (LIS) degrees are available that can be undertaken in person or via distance learning. Library apprenticeships to Level 3 have been accredited by CILIP in consultation with the Institute for Apprenticeships & Technical Education, which provide on-the-job training. CILIP also offers Certification, Chartership and Fellowship as professional qualifications, requiring submission of a portfolio of evidence. These professional qualifications do not require academic qualifications for achievement.

It is interesting to note that the Great School Libraries campaign National Survey 2019 reported that, of the schools who participated, only 34% of library staff had an academic qualification and 30% a professional qualification, with inequalities by education phase and type. Designated staff in primary and local authority-maintained schools were less likely to have relevant qualifications or training than staff in secondary or independent schools.

The library ethos

The library environment is not just a matter of its physical components, the shelving, resources and staff, nor of its location and space within the school. It also encompasses the ethos and atmosphere that is created by the synergy of its parts, its use within the school community and how it is viewed and supported by both the SMT and the staff. Everything in the library contributes to this: lighting; colour; signage; posters; displays; resources; technology; and activities. First impressions are important, as is what can be seen by students before they even walk through the doors (for example, signage, wall displays and posters outside the library). This impression should be one of a welcoming space that looks interesting and exciting and that entices students to explore further. Look at the library from the point of view of a student, someone who is walking past and glimpses inside or someone who has just entered the room – consider what there is to interest them and what visual elements there are that would encourage them to venture further or linger longer. The school library should be a hub of delightful discovery and learning, somewhere that is relevant to every student, supporting them in their reading, their learning and their aspirations.

Posters play an essential part in this. They should be visible not only in the library but also outside, around the school and in various areas that are frequented by students, such as busy corridors, toilets and the canteen. Posters are an excellent way of promoting what the library can offer by way of resources, services and activities.

Displays also serve an important purpose. They allow you to promote sections of the stock, such as specific genres and authors or new books. Displays are excellent for linking with curriculum topics being studied – use both fiction and non-fiction books in displays to encourage reading across the curriculum – and can tie in with local and national events, such as regional book awards or the Yoto Carnegie and Kate Greenaway Medals (previously the CILIP Carnegie and Kate Greenaway Children's Book Awards), Pride Month, Earth Overshoot Day or Mental Health Awareness week. It is important to change displays regularly to maintain students' interest; the easiest way to do this is to create a programme of displays for the whole year, using free resources available online and relevant items within the library collection. There are many sources of display material available and organisations and charities often provide downloadable resources to support their work and activities. Publishers can supply book posters, although it is important to ensure the books being promoted are stocked within the library as students will usually ask for them.

The librarian plays an essential role in creating the atmosphere within the school library and should cultivate a welcoming and non-judgemental space that offers students a safe area for them to explore their reading and pursue their interests, regardless of how esoteric these may be. For many students, the library is a refuge, a place they can escape to and recharge when they are struggling with a busy and demanding school day. The wellbeing aspect of the school library is undervalued and often not recognised; this is explored further in Chapter 7: Equality, Diversity and Inclusion in the School Library. A school librarian's day is always busy with a constant stream of students, requests, tasks and a never-ending to-do list; nevertheless, there will be times when the pastoral role will take over and you may find yourself abandoning your list. It is important to recognise that this is an essential part of the position and necessary if you want students to feel welcomed and that they belong in the library.

Library events and activities add to the overall ethos. These should be run throughout the year and be varied so they appeal to a wide range of students. For example, if you organise book groups, these are only likely to attract your readers; if all your competitions are writing-based, this excludes students who are more visually creative. Whether activities are regular weekly happenings or annual undertakings, they will create a dynamic space that helps to develop ownership of the library, encourage student participation and generate input into the library's future direction.

The use of the school library

The function of the library within a school needs to be clearly established as it is likely you will come across different viewpoints regarding this. The overall ethos of the school will affect how the library is used; some schools regard the space as simply supporting the English department in their quest for improving the reading skills of students, other schools will see it as a more academic space, for use by students studying and learning, and will discourage any activities that appear to be frivolous and noisy. The library is there to support the varied needs of the whole school community; these will include reading skills and studying, but should also link with students' interests and wider national and global events that inform their knowledge. In primary schools, most libraries support the development of reading skills and curriculum topics being taught by individual teachers within the classroom, supplementing existing classroom libraries. In secondary schools, many librarians have the opportunity to provide extracurricular resources and activities that extend the role of the library.

The use of the library varies from school to school. Although it is usual for primary school teachers to take their classes to the library to change books, some schools will send small groups of students with a teaching assistant and those that have librarians may well send students unaccompanied. It is also often found that older KS2 (Years 5–6) students are allowed extra responsibility and freedom to go to the library on their own and to use it at breaktimes. Many secondary schools have regular library lessons within the English timetable, at least for KS3 students. These classes are usually accompanied by a teacher and are used to browse, choose books, read silently or undertake library and book-related activities. Sometimes the librarian will be responsible for the content of these lessons, whilst in other schools, the accompanying teacher will plan them. Classes may also have research lessons in the library, booked on an ad hoc or regular basis throughout the year by various subject teachers.

The use of the library impacts on the work of the librarian and contributes to the library ethos, particularly if it is used as a classroom with no librarian or library resource input, closed to hold meetings or as a place to put disruptive students that have been removed from lessons. It is therefore important to establish rules for booking and using the library. When it is taken over for alternative practices, these create barriers and prevent the space from being a whole school resource available to the school community.

Action points

1 What is the first impression of your library when you walk through the door? Does it look interesting and attractive to students and are there displays that would encourage them to explore the space further?
2 What national events are celebrated within the school? Can you link in with these via a display or related activity?
3 Consider the layout of your library. Are there any areas that could be improved? What would be needed to make these changes and what benefits would they bring?
4 What is the labelling in your library like? Is it clear and easy to understand? Could it be improved to facilitate access to the resources?

Further reading

Dewe, M. and Duncan, S. (2018) *Design for All Reasons: Creating the Environment for the Primary School Library*, SLA.

Opening the Book (n.d.) *Designing the School Library: Articles, Reports and Guidelines*, www.designinglibraries.org.uk/?PageID=89.

Softlink (2019) *Ideas for Reviving the School Library Space*, www.softlinkint.com/blog/ideas-for-reviving-the-school-library-space.

3

Behaviour: Creating a Calm Working Environment
Sarah Pavey

Introduction

In this chapter, we will learn about creating an ambient environment that supports the use of our library space by all our school community. We will consider how and why disruption may occur occasionally and how we can resolve it calmly and assertively so that it does not impact on other users of our service.

Maybe you have a family of your own. Maybe you have experience of working with children. Maybe this role presents a whole new scenario for you and possibly, in a secondary school environment, you are not much older than some of your students. Behavioural issues with students can be stressful at times and although working in a school library is fun, this is only if we feel able to do our job effectively and within a safe environment. The good news is that most students will behave well; some may cause minor disruptions at times but only a handful will require serious intervention (DfE, 2017). Unfortunately, it is usually these few students who are the most challenging and visible. In this chapter, we will consider why students may be disruptive, how we can address these issues to restore balance and what changes we can make to our library to ensure a calm working environment.

Why does challenging behaviour happen?

Students are not naturally naughty. As humans, we need social interactions for our wellbeing and if a child is disruptive, it is usually for a reason. They may be hungry or thirsty; they may be in pain; they may be feeling too hot or too cold; they may have been upset or angry with something or someone recently; they may be being bullied; and we should be mindful that even the weather can affect their attitude. But it might just be their brain. The part of the brain that restrains impulsive action is not fully developed until we are 25 years old (Arain et al., 2013). Children are programmed to do silly things, which is part of their lifelong learning process. Without that experience, it is difficult for them to understand why appropriate behaviour is expected. Most students will already have learned acceptable social norms growing up within their home and be 'school ready', but some will not have had a role model and this can lead to challenging behaviour.

In general, students who misbehave:

- are unhappy, unwilling or unable to work
- have achieved less praise for their work
- have specific learning difficulties or are underachieving
- have poor social skills
- have low self-esteem
- are emotionally volatile
- are easily hurt or upset by others.

However, a sudden behaviour incident may also arise as a reaction to a stressful situation. When we are stressed, angry or feeling uncomfortable, it causes levels of a chemical called adrenaline in our body to rise. This places us on high alert and brings basic instincts into action. We naturally will want to run away or fight the situation we are in that causes us distress. When a student is under the influence of raised adrenaline levels, they will not be able to listen to what we tell them or predict what might happen in the future as a consequence of their actions. They may be prone to a sudden impulsive response. Sometimes, we might meet these students while being unaware of their situation and can inadvertently trigger a behavioural incident.

Here's an example – Sam got out on the wrong side of the bed. First, there was a massive row at home because he could not find his school shoes and so he put on trainers. He stormed out without breakfast. He was pulled up for his footwear on arrival at school and given a detention. He was in such a state when he arrived for his first lesson that he dropped his bag, which contained a drink that then spilt all over his friend's books resulting in a swearing match. The teacher sent him to the Headteacher because he swore at her too. He was sent back to his next lesson at the end of the period and told to report back to the Headteacher at the end of the day. He then wanders into your library at breaktime and knocks over a display stand ...

The difficulty is that raised levels of adrenaline can last for 90 minutes. It is like a firework that has failed to ignite and if we return to it too soon it can explode unexpectedly. In schools, there is rarely time for a 90-minute time out and teenagers can be impulsive. We can now see how a 'bad day' can escalate from a minor incident to an exclusion level very quickly. We need to be mindful of these possibilities, but conversely, we should not be offering our library as a sanctuary for students who have misbehaved. Most students need the library and its services to be available to them and to provide an atmosphere conducive to work and leisure activities. We should be wary of promoting the idea that the library is a detention centre for those who have broken the school rules.

Challenging behaviour can also arise through poor communication. Our students are not mini adults – they are children. As such, they have a limited experience of life and social situations. When we speak with people, we base what we say to them on our own perspectives. That perception is built from our experiences, our moral standards and expectations. The other participants in the conversation will reply based on their own values. If those viewpoints differ there may be an argument. However, if we try to understand where other people are coming from then we can have a constructive discussion. With students, we need to appreciate that their perspective on a situation may be very different to ours – they often have different priorities because they have no experience of the consequences. We also need to be mindful of our own language.

Librarian: Lucy, can you please leave your bag in the locker area.
Lucy: I can't, Miss.
Librarian: What do you mean you can't? Of course you can. Just go and put it away.
Lucy: I've got things in it I need.
Librarian: Don't be stupid. Just go and put it in the locker.
Lucy: Don't call me stupid.
Librarian: Look, just go and put the bag in the locker.
Lucy: No, I won't. You can't make me.
Librarian: Right, that is it. You are going straight to the Headteacher.
Lucy (to her friends who are listening): Silly cow!

How could this have been handled better? Maybe Lucy did have items in her bag she needed for her own personal reasons. Nonetheless, there may have been a no bags policy in the library for health and safety reasons, for example, to avoid tripping over bulky holdalls on the floor. Perhaps the librarian needed to take Lucy to one side and find out the reason behind her defiance. This scenario also illustrates another common communication problem as Lucy was quite disrespectful to the librarian in the language she used. Sometimes, students have not yet learned how to adapt their tone and speech according to the person they are addressing, which could be because their home environment has not nurtured these social skills (Behaviour2Learn, 2011). As a result, they may communicate with people in authority in the same way that they would their friends. Inevitably, this causes resentment and hostility.

Remember, students tend to misbehave for a reason. It might be to gain peer approval, to gain attention, to avoid work or because they are not used to adults setting boundaries. Dreikurs, Grunwald and Pepper (2013) identified four goals of misbehaviour, outlined below.

Attention goal

Zoe knew that if she opened her packet of crisps noisily under the table, the librarian would be over in a shot. The librarian heard the noise and thought 'Oh no, here we go again'. He asked Zoe to stop, and she did, but she then tried to start a personal conversation. The librarian said he was busy and as soon as his back was turned, Zoe was munching again. He returned and asked her to hand over the crisps. The packet was empty. As soon as the librarian returned to his desk, he heard another packet being opened. This time, he ignored it. Zoe, realising he was not coming over again, stopped, and put the crisps away. When Zoe left the library, the librarian took her to one side and praised her for having the sense to put the bag away by herself without the need to be told. Zoe would learn that she gets rewarded for not attracting attention in an unwanted manner.

Power goal

Josh was reading his book at breaktime. The issue was that Josh had managed to spread himself and his belongings over three of the comfy chairs in the reading corner. The librarian asked him to move slightly so that others could use the space. Josh refused, saying, 'Look, I am reading my book quietly and now you are disturbing me. This is a library and it is here for reading and these others probably won't be behaving as well as I am.' Again, the librarian suggests that he moves up. Josh gets angry, saying, 'Here we go again, you are not even respecting your own rules.' At this point, the librarian was exasperated by Josh's attitude and wanted to get him out of the library altogether. But then she reflected and said, 'Oh Josh, you are one of my best library users, I wondered if you could help me with something where I need a knowledgeable person. Leave your things for a minute and come with me.' Here we can see how the librarian has distracted Josh from his dominance over the issue and yet kept his alliance.

Revenge goal

Amit had been so badly behaved one breaktime the previous week that the librarian had asked him to leave the library. He had been constantly annoying others, preventing them from working and reading and they had complained about him. Amit was not happy about this. Amit storms back into the library and starts randomly pulling books off the shelves and leaving them all over the room. The librarian asks him to stop but Amit just shouts, 'You hate me, you have it in for me, so it doesn't matter what I do.' Then, he upsets a chess set all over the floor. The librarian thinks, 'Why is he over-reacting like this? I am not going to let him get away with this,' and says, 'Right get out … NOW!' Amit retorts, 'See, I know you hate me and you don't want me in here.' The next time Amit returns ready to wreak revenge, the librarian takes him aside for a word, sits him down in the office and tries to understand what is making him feel he is being unfairly treated. They can work out how to resolve the issue together and avoid him being excluded from the library again.

Display of inadequacy goal

Nadia is crying in a corner of the library on her own again. The librarian moves over to her and wearily asks what is wrong. Nadia says she is so useless and worthless at everything she does. The librarian makes helpful suggestions but every one of them is rejected by Nadia for various reasons. The librarian despairs at the situation and is exhausted by the constant effort and guilt of having such an unhappy child in the library. Nadia, not having had any reprimand for this behaviour, or action on her part requested, continues along the same track. The librarian changes tack and asks Nadia about life outside school. It turns out she has a puppy at home and is training it. The librarian praises her for what must be a difficult job that not everyone would have the patience to see through. The librarian is not sympathising with Nadia's current situation but, through finding alternatives, can raise her self-esteem and get her to refocus, away from the negative attention seeking behaviour pattern.

Some students may have recognised learning difficulties or special needs and this can affect how they behave towards us and others in the library. Within a lesson, the teacher will be aware of this, or the student will have a support worker, but in breaktimes these students often choose to visit the library as a place of sanctuary, knowing there will be an adult present to help and/or protect them. The difficulty may be that during these times we have different rules concerning behaviour and this can pose challenges for these students. We should try and familiarise ourselves with the special needs register and, if possible, attend any staff meetings where concerns about students are raised so we are aware of special circumstances.

A student with Attention Deficit Hyperactivity Disorder (ADHD) or who is on the autism spectrum CAN'T conform but generally they will want to. If we confront them for running around in the library, they will be confused and not understand what they did wrong. We can create opportunities for ADHD students, for example, to shout 'Library will close in 5 minutes' or getting them to run an errand as a chance for them to get up and about. We could keep fidget toys at the library desk for students to borrow or invest in special seat cushions to loan out that address ADHD needs and keep these students calm. For those with autism or Asperger's Syndrome, we must ensure they have understood what the behaviour rules look like in practice.

A student with Oppositional Defiant Disorder (ODD) WON'T conform unless it is on their terms. These students will claim victimisation and try to place the blame for their behaviour on you. For example, if you caution them for speaking too loudly, they will accuse you of singling them out and then will suggest they were only having to raise their voice because you were not in control of library noise levels. With these students, we need to be firm but fair and be willing to be flexible. We should avoid shouting back at them, respect their personal space, keep our body language neutral and take them aside privately to discuss the issue. We should not relate to previous incidents with these students as that can fuel the flames of the argument.

Perhaps the most difficult students are those with a Conduct Disorder (CD). These students DON'T CARE about their behaviour or its consequences and appear to have a different agenda altogether. This might be the student you have a word with for deliberately ripping pages out of books instead of copying from them. These are often the students who are in serious violation of rules, who are caught stealing or are destructive or aggressive. We can try and build a relationship of respect and model good behaviour to them. We need to decide what we should deal with and what can be let go. Once we identify this primary need, we should address it and move on while staying calm. We may need to ask for help from senior leaders or a colleague in dealing with these incidents.

There are many different types of special needs and it is time well spent to discuss the behavioural nuances with the learning support department to find out about specific strategies they recommend. By keeping the way behaviour is addressed consistent for these students, it can help their control and response.

So, we understand that disruptive behaviour may manifest for various reasons and we have seen how it might be dealt with within these scenarios. But how do we deal with behaviour more generally?

Managing disruptive behaviour

Setting the rules

We can learn a great deal from our teaching colleagues and it is useful if we can observe positive role models in action. Most teachers will begin their lessons calmly, with a routine. This might involve lining students up outside a classroom before entering, meeting and greeting at the door by name, or a call and response at the beginning of a lesson to underpin the behaviour expectations. The school behaviour rules may be displayed prominently on the classroom wall. During the year, the teacher learns about the students as individuals, through working with them on a regular basis.

As librarians, we are more akin to supply teachers. If a class comes to the library, it may be on a sporadic basis. The class will usually be accompanied by their regular teacher, but this then raises the question of who is responsible for student behaviour. It is important that we establish ground rules with the teacher in advance of the lesson, so clear instructions can be given to the students. If this does not happen, students may feel the situation is like two parents giving them different advice and the temptation will be to play one off against the other. We need to respect that the teacher has more knowledge of the class nuances, but if we have library rules these need to be acknowledged too and these may differ from specific classroom rules. Regardless, we should all be following the published school rules, not least because this is an inspection criterion for Ofsted (2019).

Librarians also face the dilemma that, probably uniquely in the school, the physical space is used both as a classroom and for leisure time. We need to think carefully about how we manage this to avoid mixed messages being given to students.

At the end of the day, a new student, Vikki, was in the library waiting to be picked up and quietly doing some homework. Vikki asked the librarian if she could use her phone in the library to call her mum. The school rules allowed students to phone a guardian after the end of school, so the librarian agreed. The next day the librarian caught Vikki on the phone during a library lesson and confiscated the device. Vikki was distraught, embarrassed and confused. She thought the librarian had given her permission to use the phone in the library.

It is so important that we make our rules explicit. Hopefully, we will have been allowed an induction lesson at the start of the year to set our ground rules, but then we need to be mindful of new students. Deciding on a set of specific rules for the library in addition to the school rules requires thought. Because every school is unique, we cannot just borrow from another librarian and tick the box. We need to plan what is needed in our school library so that it provides both a good working environment but also somewhere for students to relax and recharge. It is like a referee controlling a sports match – knowing what to let pass and when to blow the whistle. Too many rules and students will not engage, participate or use our library; too few and we run the risk of mayhem!

Three common rules that underpin library behaviour concern:

- library noise levels
- eating and drinking within the library
- numbers of students at breaktimes, before and after school.

A first step in deciding how we will deal with these scenarios is to consult the school rules and adhere to these as a priority. Secondly, we need to consider if our specific rules should be conditional to allow for differences between lesson time and breaktimes. Thirdly, we should think about the health and safety consequences if the rule is not applied. We should not set these rules in isolation – it is important to discuss our intentions with our line managers to ensure we are keeping to the wider aims of the school community. This is especially crucial because, as has been mentioned, behaviour is an inspection criterion. If we are taking over a role from a previous librarian, we can use our new employment status as an opportunity to reflect and, if necessary, change existing rules. Consider these scenarios:

- The students from a younger year group were playing a noisy library game as part of their library lesson. However, the space was being shared with older students who complained they could not concentrate on their revision. After the lesson, it was breaktime, and the same younger students, excited from their lesson, continued to make noise about the books they had discovered. This drove others away from the library who were looking for a quiet space.
- Water fountains had been placed around the school to ensure students were keeping hydrated but the nearest one to the library was some distance away. Some students were now filling up bottles and bringing them back to the library, which had a no eating or drinking policy.
- It was raining and the number of students trying to get into the library at lunchtime was far too many for the space. The librarian was trying to help users and the student librarians were unable to control the flood of people. It was noisy and chaotic!

When we face such dilemmas, we need to ask what we can manage ourselves, what could we manage with some support and what do we need to pass to someone more senior for resolution? We should use our line managers so that the rules we set help us to carry out our role safely and efficiently. We should not be afraid to ask for help and support when we need it.

Working with students

Once our scaffold of rules is set, we need to think about how we manage the behaviour that we see from our students. Mostly, we will be dealing with low level disruption arising from talking, movement, social interactions, relationships between students and between ourselves and our students. We should follow the school behaviour plan and stepped consequences consistently. Fundamentally, we need to remember – what we allow, we encourage.

How we are viewed by students depends upon three factors: our body language; what we say; and the tone of voice we use. The most important of these is our body language. Our non-verbal communication can help diffuse a situation without a word being said. What we say is the least important of these three factors, yet we should still be mindful of the language we choose to use. Regardless of our means of communication, there are some general pointers we can use in the management of low-level disruption:

- Always plan for good behaviour.
- Separate the inappropriate behaviour from the student.
- Focus on the primary behaviours.
- Actively build trust and support.
- Model the behaviour we wish to see.
- Be mindful of our language.
- Follow up on issues that count.

Let us consider some of these factors in more depth.

We should always make it clear that it is the behaviour that is being addressed and not the student. If we label a student as 'bad' it can confirm an already poor self-image and reduce self-esteem. The student will live up or down to their given label, so we need to offer hope and help to change their behaviour. If we have repeat offenders, we should keep a record of their names, incidents and dates in case the behaviour escalates or the information is needed to build a wider pattern of their behaviour elsewhere in the school. We can help these students to change by giving them responsibilities and praising them whenever possible. If they do change, then appropriate behaviour should ALWAYS be associated with the student, because they themselves have become empowered by making a positive choice. We can help them achieve this response firstly by making the choices explicit and then through rewards and sanctions.

We must be mindful that sanctions do not change behaviour. They need to be applied for long enough to allow a student to change their choice. Rewards do change behaviour, so praise or a tangible prize for positive action works wonders. Rewards should not be given as bribes and a reward, once given, should never be taken away.

Good manners are the social glue that help us form social groups. We can model good manners by always saying please and thank you. We can gently correct those who do not demonstrate good manners. We need to show our students the respect that we would expect for ourselves, so for example, if we have to break off working with one student to deal with another, we need to remember to apologise. This, along with a calm outward appearance in our body language and facial expression, helps maintain a pleasant atmosphere.

Our students will look to us for clues about positive attitudes too. Even if we are having the worst day ever, we need to use our acting skills and shield our emotions from them. In our mannerisms, our tone of voice and in the language we use, we should endeavour to:

- be definite, giving clear instructions
- show we are aware, so the student understands the consequences of a bad choice
- be calm and consistent so the student considers us as always being fair
- give structure to the task or lesson so the student can see the small steps
- be positive, giving lots of praise regularly so the student remains motivated
- be interested so students can see we are human
- be flexible and know when to allow a little leeway for a better outcome
- be persistent and do not give up on something we have already started
- engage with students so they can see we are keen for them to succeed.

If we model our own behaviour and expectations, we may already have created an ambient atmosphere for our library. This respect and understanding from students do not happen instantly. It takes time to nurture and grow. Even when this environment is well established, there will be incidents because, as we have seen, behaviour can be affected by all kinds of variable factors over which we have little or no control. So, what do we do to resolve any issues? Here are some ideas.

Following an established procedure that is known and understood by students
The level of noise from the library lesson was rising steadily. The librarian followed the steps in the behaviour rules that were established and agreed

by students and the librarian at the beginning of the year. The librarian issued the class a warning with a consequence. A few students did not heed this advice. The librarian moved over to each of them individually and had a quiet word, informing them of the detention they would receive if they chose not to use a quieter voice. One student, Faz, continued to disrupt, so at the end of the lesson the librarian took Faz aside and issued the detention.

This demonstrates the importance of being fair but consistent in our approach. Faz will learn that the behaviour was his choice and his responsibility.

Dealing with non-verbal disruption

At breaktime, Asha was trying to attract the attention of a boy she fancied by deliberately giggling with her friend and glancing over at him. The librarian asked Asha to concentrate on her reading and reminded her of the library behaviour rules even at breaktime. Asha responded with eye rolling and much flicking of her hair. The librarian decided to let it pass and Asha stopped. However, a short time later, the original behaviour resumed. This time, the librarian asked Asha quietly to come to the office where she had a quiet word to establish ground rules and to explain that the library could not be used in this way.

This librarian hoped the situation would resolve itself, but when the poor behaviour resumed, it was important for the message to be given away from an audience so that Asha would listen and understand rather than trying to impress her friends with a 'cool' attitude.

Using verbal strategies

During the lesson, the librarian noticed that Temi was out of his seat again, bothering students at the other tables. The librarian moved to talk to him but as ever he was full of excuses for his actions, claiming he was doing work. He even stated he was glad the librarian had come over because he wanted to ask a specific question about a resource. The librarian confirmed what Temi said and then issued a directive: 'Temi, maybe you were visiting that table to discuss work AND now I want you to return to your own space and carry on with your work there. Thank you.'

This is a powerful tactic because it defuses conflict by seeming to agree with the student. By using the word 'and', the compliance is more readily acceptable. This approach minimises the potential for getting into arguments. It allows us to move on and regain the momentum of the lesson.

We need to make positive responses when requiring good behaviour, indicating this is what we expect:

- 'Terry, stand still and wait your turn, thank you.' NOT: 'Terry, stop pushing or you will go to the back of the queue.'
- 'Greta, I need you to choose to face the front and listen, thank you.' NOT: 'Greta, stop talking and pay attention.'
- 'Zak, remember to walk calmly around the library, thank you.' NOT: 'OI, YOU, STOP RUNNING!'

It is useful for us to practice making statements rather than asking questions and assuming students will comply with our request. Never ask a question unless we really want to hear the answer. To give an example: the librarian was sure that Leanne had just sworn at her and without thinking asked Leanne, 'What did you say?' and the answer was … Well, you can imagine!

There are many tactics we can use both in lesson time and breaktime to gain control and send a signal to students or to issue a directive. If we need silence to issue a directive, we can use a visual signal by adopting a pose and a look that students will notice, such as crossing our arms or staring. Or we might choose to use a physical signal, such as a timer, stop clock or giant egg timer or display a traffic light system or electronic timer on a whiteboard. We can give an audio signal using clapping, bells, whistles or a 1-2-3 countdown, or we might use a kinaesthetic response by asking students to raise their hands, copying as we raise ours, indicating we need their attention.

Within lessons, it is important to retain control. Part of this involves communicating our expectations of when activity is to take place and when to stop. We can use some of the signals already suggested. Students find it difficult to judge time, as do we all if we are absorbed by a task, so playing music is another useful technique to signal the end of time for an activity when the music stops.

When students do not comply, we can use repetition (the gramophone record approach) to give some leeway and we should not be afraid to use humour to coax them back on task. It is important to have empathy and to try and see the students' viewpoint if there is a conflict brewing. However, whilst we can be reasonable with our students, we should not reason with them.

Managing serious behaviour issues

As we have noted, serious and dangerous behaviour issues are rare. We need to keep ourselves and students safe and, if an incident of this nature occurs, we need to find help to deal with it. It is very unlikely that the situation we face has originated in the library; it is more likely to be an accumulative effect from something that happened previously in the day. Typically, this may happen when a student is tired or hungry, so certain times of the day are more likely to be a flashpoint. Unfortunately, this is often when the library is at its busiest. How do we handle this?

Firstly, we need to remove any physical objects or other students from the arena. We need to move the offender to a quiet space or ask them to step outside. We can send another student to fetch help. The remaining students will probably be shocked and compliant if you have this under control.

Once the disruptive student has calmed down, if help has still not arrived, move them to a separate quiet space and try – in a neutral, low and calm voice and giving them plenty of personal space – to let them tell you their version of events. Wait for them to tell you, do not probe. In response, use their name and agree with them anything that is factually correct, but do not pass judgement or comment on other aspects. Do not refer to the past or the future. We do not have to make eye contact. Sometimes giving them a sweet can help them feel better, especially if they might be hungry.

Hopefully, by now, we will have support. We should be mindful of the natural after-effects following incidents of this kind. We will feel upset and shaky, and we too will need some time out. Once we are feeling calmer, we can record what happened and name the student and any witnesses. It is important that if the student returns, we make it clear to them that we do not hold a grudge. It is useful to talk the incident over with colleagues when we have experienced such a shock – this helps our own mental wellbeing and gives us confidence to face the student again.

In summary

No one is perfect when it comes to behaviour management. It is not predictable, but we can lessen the risk of both low-level disruption and more serious outbursts if we remember:

- we CANNOT directly control the behaviour of students, but we CAN control some of those things that lead to poor behaviour and show them that behaviour is their choice
- we have LITTLE CONTROL over external factors – such as poor housing, lack of parenting skills or family issues – that may be affecting the student
- we have 100% CONTROL over how we choose to respond emotionally to the behaviour of students.

We also have three basic rights: (1) to be safe; (2) to carry out our role effectively; and (3) to be treated with dignity and respect.

It is important for us to maintain emotional balance in busy and fast-moving education settings. When we are calm and rational, we are most effective. We can use our own emotions as a model for students to follow. We do not want to be so controlling that we are unapproachable. However, we are not their friend and do not want to run the risk of being taken advantage of. Tough love is a good approach. Here, we acknowledge:

- it is our job to set the boundaries
- students may test those boundaries
- students make mistakes in their behaviour – that is normal and healthy
- students need to be helped to experience achievement
- caring means saying 'no' and meaning 'no' at the right time
- there is always more to a young person than their behaviour problem.

We want our students to learn boundaries with dignity, but at the same time understand the effects of risk taking and motivation through praise. We need to be mindful that confrontation makes poor behaviour worse. If we want to see good behaviour, we must teach it to our students according to their needs.

Action points

1 Ensure that the school behaviour code is displayed in your library.
2 Revise your school library behaviour policy with your line manager and, if possible, with representative students for both lesson time and leisure time.
3 Be aware of who you can contact in an emergency.
4 Find out which students are registered as having special needs and discuss behavioural policy with your SENCo.
5 Consider how you will communicate acceptable noise levels to library users.

Creating a Reading Rich Environment

Annie Everall

Introduction

As a school librarian, you will have a passion for reading; a passion that you will want to share with your school community. You will want them to be passionate about reading and to talk about and promote books and reading. You will want that passion to emanate from the library, permeate the school and demonstrate in different ways that the school has a strong reading culture and creates a reading rich environment for all. This chapter aims to support you in this and covers the following topics:

- the role of the school librarian in creating a reading rich environment in school
- finding out about activities and promotions that could be run in your library
- national book initiatives
- national and local book awards
- practical ideas for creating a reading rich environment
- author events
- the rights of the reader
- funding sources
- working with other school staff
- Schools Library Services
- follow up activities
- references and further information.

The school librarian and the reading environment in school

Ask anybody who works with children or who cares about the future of young people and they will agree one thing: reading is the most basic of basics. The child who reads is a successful child: more likely to succeed academically; more likely to succeed socially; and more likely to be inquisitive about the world around them, maybe even to feel empowered to try to change it for the better. This is not just my opinion. It is a judgement supported by a body as influential as the Organisation for Economic Co-operation and Development (OECD).

When you read often, when it is as effortless and integral to your being as eating, drinking, sleeping, and breathing, you are able to empathise. To access and order information, to interpret and explore the world around you.

(Gibbons, 2011)

Without the sunlight of literature children cannot grow as they should. We know that from books come knowledge and understanding, that they are a source of infinite joy and fun, that they stimulate imagination and creativity, that they open eyes and minds and hearts. It is through the power and music and magic of stories and poems that children can expand their own intellectual curiosity, develop the empathy and awareness that they will need to tackle the complexities of their own emotions, of the human condition in which they find themselves. And it's through books that we can learn the mastery of words, the essential skill that will enable us to express ourselves well enough to achieve our potential in the classroom and beyond.

(Morpurgo, 2009)

These two quotes by Alan Gibbons and Michael Morpurgo demonstrate what we all know: that books can inspire children and foster their love of reading, can help stimulate their curiosity to learn new facts, explore or come to terms with situations they are dealing with in their lives, as well as supporting their growth and development.

Librarians are the heart of a school's reading environment. They can lead by example, creating a ripple effect that travels out of the library via the students and staff and permeates across the school. The library is in a unique position and by working with the English department to identify struggling or reluctant readers, the school library can have a measurable impact on enthusiasm and reading attainment. Reporting on this to senior leadership can help demonstrate the work of the school library and hopefully ensure adequate funding to continue to inspire lifelong readers. So where should a new school librarian start?

As Alex Williams says in *Get Everyone Reading – A Primer on Reading for Pleasure*:

You can't create a reading culture. Not by yourself. But you can and should help to make it happen. The short and longer answer to how to create a reading culture is: 'all the other sections of this guide' (a thriving library, great books, reading aloud, teacher role models, reading events, following children's own choices, and so on).

(Williams, 2021, 12)

Your starting point should be your library environment – this is explored in more detail in Chapter 2: The Library Environment. Your library needs to be fantastic; it should be exciting, attractive, welcoming and a place that students want to go. Keep it up to date with a diverse range of resources that are well presented. You need to find ways to promote and market the library to students and staff and to get them to do that on your behalf too. Your aim is to make every student want to read and promote the library. You can do this by giving them a stake in it – buy books they request (within reason), talk with them and listen to their suggestions for activities, events and clubs or promotional displays.

As the school librarian, what should you do personally? One of the best pieces of advice we can give a new school librarian is READ, READ, READ, DISCUSS AND PROMOTE! Librarians need to read what the children and young people are reading so that they can recommend books that suit the needs of each student, but also to give depth to discussions with students about books. A good starting point is to find out what reading scheme is being used in your school and talk to staff about ways in which the library can support reading development. Work with staff and families to encourage everyone to read more. Involve the whole school in developing the reading culture and creating a reading rich environment.

Be visible in your own reading and encourage other staff to do the same. Read about books too – social media can be very useful here, but also sign up for relevant newsgroups and publishers' and library suppliers' newsletters. Work at keeping your own reading knowledge up to date. Websites such as Booktrust (www.booktrust.org.uk) and LoveReading4Kids (www.lovereading4kids. co.uk) can provide useful information, as well as opening extracts for newly released titles.

Finding out about activities and promotions that could be run in your library

Find out what events and activities will be happening during the forthcoming year that your school could get involved with. Look for ways that you can link activities and initiatives into the curriculum. As well as keeping a watch on social media, announcements in the press and through websites mentioned in this book, there are key resources that can help you find out about other activities and promotions, as well as help support your own professional knowledge and development. More information on these can be found in Chapter 10: Moving on: CPD and Qualifications.

The following websites highlight some of the major events that take place during the year:

- The School Reading List: https://schoolreadinglist.co.uk/competitions-for-children/childrens-book-festivals-events-and-competitions
- Booktrust: www.booktrust.org.uk/books-and-reading/events
- LIPSSEE: https://preplibs.wordpress.com/?s=events

Work with other staff to create your own school calendar of events that you can celebrate, involving the whole school. Ask your pupil library assistants to promote your events to classes and design posters to promote them. The school timetable is packed full, so think of activities that don't interfere with this too much or that can be done for 10 minutes a day or as homework. The Great School Libraries website has a wealth of information and support for school librarians. These include a range of case studies on different themes such as reading for pleasure (www.greatschoollibraries.org.uk/case-studies).

National book initiatives

Throughout the year, there are key national book-related activities and celebrations that take place. These offer opportunities for a school librarian to celebrate them and use them as a focal point for bringing the whole school together to promote literacy and reading, through displays, a programme of activities, author events or a specific project. These can be a good starting point for a new school librarian to engage with. By incorporating national events such as World Book Day and National Poetry Day into the school calendar, the school librarian can provide opportunities for the entire school community to engage with books and reading. It is often events such as these that spark the beginning of a reading community. In particular, World Book Day provides opportunities for author visits, distribution of World Book Day National Book Tokens and book-related activities and competitions. Some of the major initiatives are listed in Appendix 2, but there are others that you should explore.

National and local book awards

There are a growing number of children's book awards, both national and local. For a new school librarian, familiarising yourself with these can have several benefits. They are a great way to discover new books that you may wish to purchase for the school library. Aim to create partnerships with your local public library services, as well as other school librarians, to help you gain knowledge of local book awards and literary festivals and build your networks. In addition, some of the awards provide opportunities for schools to participate, such as shadowing the Yoto Carnegie and Kate Greenaway Medals. This can provide a rich and rewarding experience for students, offering an effective way for them to engage in reading for pleasure and develop the habit of talking about the books they read. It can also provide purpose and focus for school reading groups. Toppsta (https://toppsta.com) outlines most of the major national children's book awards and their parameters, as well as details of the shortlists and winners. Some of the key national awards are included in Appendix 3.

Practical Ideas for creating a reading rich environment

One of the best ways of getting ideas for strategies and initiatives to try in your school library is to build your own knowledge by undertaking wider CPD through reading, seeking out articles and exploring relevant websites. The Open University Reading for Pleasure website (https://ourfp.org) has lots of useful activities that have been tried and tested in the library and classroom. Although mainly aimed at primary level, they could easily be used for secondary schools. The Great School Libraries website (www.greatschoollibraries.org.uk) has information and case studies and is a valuable resource for new school librarians.

It can also be useful to talk to other colleagues in your school library networks and 'magpie' their ideas. Share ideas that work for you too, so that others can benefit from your knowledge, experiences and successes. Consider working with other schools in your area on joint initiatives. Organisations such as CILIP School Libraries Group, the Reading Agency, the National Literacy Trust and the School Library Association provide resources and examples of reading initiatives successfully running in schools. Remember, too, that even if you try something and it doesn't work as successfully as hoped, you can still learn from it and revise it to make it work more successfully next time.

By looking at your school's strategic development plan, and surveying staff and students, you can look for areas where the library can enrich and support the school community. For example, if there is a need for increased wellbeing provision in the school, the library can link to this by purchasing and promoting self-care books and activities.

When you are trying to develop a reading culture and create a reading rich environment, whether in primary or secondary schools, look at all aspects of literature, such as events, creative activities and different formats of books and materials. Also, look at all ages and key stages of school, as well as all reading ability levels, to ensure that you are providing something for everyone. Talk to students and find out what they would like the library to organise. Whatever initiatives you engage in, remember to build in some form of evaluation, such as measuring loan increases, so that you can include this in your annual report.

The following are all practical ideas and tips that have been developed and used successfully by school librarian Zoe Rowley from Wolverhampton Grammar School, members of the CILIP School Libraries Group national committee, the collaborators on this book, and others whose articles are referenced in this chapter.

Book awards
- Shadowing a book award can give focus and purpose to a school book club or reading group. Many awards will have lots of activity and discussion ideas for shadowing groups on their websites.
- Whichever award you are shadowing across the school, aim to ensure that each book is championed by at least one member of staff. You can also get those staff to talk to the children and tell them why they are championing that book.
- Work with other librarians in your area and participate in your local book award if there is one.
- When shadowing a book award, put a set of the books in the staff room for staff to borrow, to read themselves or to read to their class. Discuss the books with them.
- Book champions – get children in teams to devise a 'selling' campaign for an allocated title from the book award list and get them to present it to a judge or team of judges. If it is a multi-school award, each school can be allocated a different book.

Reading champions and reading buddies
- Reading buddies – pair less able readers with an older reading mentor (such as Year 7/8 with Year 10/11). Students come to the library at form

time and the older ones can model reading to the younger ones and talk about the book they are sharing.

- Alternatively, students in Year 10/11 can choose a book for those in Year 8/9, which they can all read as a group and then break into small groups to discuss.
- Reading Champions – students can promote books to the wider school in various ways. Pupil library assistants can be used very successfully with this. You can find ways of making this happen, such as a 'favourites' display or by students going into different classrooms to 'push' books via a 'booktalking' slot.

Book clubs and reading groups

- By opening the library at break, lunchtimes and after school, you can provide a safe inclusive space for students to come and visit. During this time, the library can be a fantastic location to run book clubs, reading groups, debates, book-related craft activities or story time sessions. Think about what might work best for your different audiences, such as confident readers who want to be stretched or less able readers who want to be supported.
- Chatterbooks is the Reading Agency's network of children's reading clubs run in public libraries and schools to encourage reading for pleasure (https://readingagency.org.uk/children/quick-guides/chatterbooks).
- Book review clubs – get students to read new books that you have added to the library and then write a review or make a video of themselves verbally reviewing the book. This can be put up as a display in the library, on the library management system (LMS), if that is possible, or on digital screens across the school. It may also be worth contacting publishers to see if they are able to provide proof copies of books before publication so your students can write a review for the publisher.
- Try holding a different kind of book club, such as a research club or a newspaper club where students can become reporters and create a termly school newspaper. Book clubs can also be focused on a specific genre or format, for example, manga or anime, graphic novels, fantasy or murder/mystery.
- Premier League Reading Stars (https://plprimarystars.com/resources/reading-stars-pack), developed by the National Literacy Trust, is an evidence-based and effective recovery reading intervention for students who might not enjoy reading but do enjoy football. It supports students to read a wide range of formats about the subject they love.

- School breakfast clubs have been turned into breakfast book clubs via grants from Give a Book (http://giveabook.org.uk). One school made their breakfast club into a very popular family breakfast reading club, where some of the most socially deprived families could have breakfast and read together. Parent and child reading groups, either before or after school, can also encourage further reading at home.
- Start a staff reading group by getting teachers and support staff to read and discuss children's and young adult books.
- It's always worth checking out publishers' websites for books that you are going to be reading in your group as they will often have resources to support titles, including discussion questions and activities.

Visible reading

- Be visible in your own reading and encourage staff to do the same.
- Encourage staff to display their current reading in their teaching rooms, either by having an A4 laminated poster that says 'I am currently reading' with a book cover that can be changed, or by having the book they are currently reading on a display stand on the desk.
- Put up posters of celebrities reading, around the school as well as in the library.
- Use notice boards to promote reading, both in the library and around the school.
- Ask staff to talk about the books they are reading in assemblies – this can be particularly good if male teachers get involved or for subjects like science or PE. It can be a good way to link in with World Book Day, Science Week or a major sporting event.
- Display poems chosen by staff around the school to link to National Poetry Day.
- Video staff reading and talking about the books they are reading and show the videos in assembly or on screens around the school. Get the Head of English, SLT and the Literacy Co-ordinator to encourage all staff to participate.
- A simple and effective way to encourage visible reading across the school is to timetable 10 minutes of Drop Everything and Read (DEAR) time each week. This not only provides time for students to read independently, but it also allows children to see their participating teachers as positive reading role models. If that is a step too far initially, try it for a specific initiative such as World Book Day, have one tutor time a week devoted to reading or run a DEAR session with a specific year group.

By running such initiatives and seeing a measurable increase in reading for pleasure, the library will become an essential resource.

Book events and activities

- Holding a school Book Week can be a good opportunity to really focus on reading for pleasure and for information. Invite authors to visit virtually or in person, hold poetry workshops or slams, rap writing workshops, bookmaking workshops, information book sessions with authors or reading assemblies.
- Book quizzes can be fun; either a school quiz with locally devised questions or work with other local librarians to devise a regional quiz.
- Whole school reading programme – give all tutors a box of books from the library and have students read first thing in the morning during form time. Swap the boxes halfway through the year if more books are needed.
- Participate in the Bookbuzz programme for Years 7 and 8 – a reading programme from Booktrust that aims to help schools inspire a love of reading in 11 to 13-year-olds (www.booktrust.org.uk/what-we-do/programmes-and-campaigns/bookbuzz).
- Create reader profiles for all new Year 7 students and then keep a log of their reading journey to encourage the reading of more challenging texts as they progress through school.
- Hold a yearly overnight readathon, where students are sponsored to stay overnight in school and the school attempts to have someone reading all night. This can be great fun, raise money for library funds and result in many children finding a new favourite author.
- Run an in-house summer reading challenge, encouraging students to read one or two books a week over the holidays and then quiz them using Accelerated Reader in the first week back. Give them a small prize if they pass at least six quizzes. You can also use the national Summer Reading Challenge to save re-inventing the wheel.
- Use digital encouragement as well. Put QR codes inside book covers that lead students to a book trailer or play trailers on a big screen in the library and/or across the school.
- Make a book. Each class writes stories in the style of a favourite author. Selected ones are collected into a self-published book (which the librarian will need to copy edit). Another option that has worked successfully in primary schools is to get the whole school to write a collective book. Each class from Nursery to Year 6 works on two or three paragraphs together. You supply the first sentence or two. Tell each class

what the story is about and the names of the main characters. Another opportunity to get children writing is to participate in The Write Path initiative. This is an international collaborative writing programme enabling children to add paragraphs to stories started by leading children's authors (www.bevhumphrey.com/the-write-path.html).

- Fathers Reading Week – a week of celebrations of father/male role models, available as a case study on the Great School Libraries website (www.greatschoollibraries.org.uk/reading-for-pleasure-information).
- Father's Day event – an after school event for fathers/carers and children with library activities, a reading tent, shared stories, a storyteller from the public library, a stand for the public library to promote itself and sign up parents and children, and a male author visit. This could also be done for Mother's Day.
- Cinema night – choose a film of a popular book and ask the teacher of the classes attending to read the book aloud to students beforehand. Remember to check out licensing agreements before showing the film (https://copyrightandschools.org/film).

Early years activities that work well:

- Visit the Nursery class (or invite them to visit the library every week) and read or tell stories to them. Use props (dolls, animals, artefacts) and costumes to enliven the stories. Story sacks containing a picture book and several story props, artefacts and costumes can be borrowed from some Schools Library Services by subscribing schools.
- Ask children to make up their own stories. Give them a theme, write down the story they tell you and stick it into a scrapbook. Ask the children to draw pictures related to their stories and stick them in too. When this is finished, add it to their classroom collection.

Emma Suffield, School Librarian at St Wilfred's Academy, and a previous School Librarian of the Year, has some innovative ideas to get students reading:

- Golden Tickets – 'I place six golden tickets in books that haven't been taken out in a while. If a student reads a book containing a ticket, they are asked to write a short summary about it to win a prize.'
- Get Caught Reading Raffle – 'When students are "caught" reading silently in the library during break and lunchtimes, they are issued with a raffle ticket by one of our student librarians. At the end of every half term, the raffle is drawn and the winner receives a goodie bag of

reading-related materials. Students can be entered as many times as they want, but only once a day. This is a great initiative to encourage students to use the LRC (Learning Resource Centre) for reading during break and lunch.'

- Twitter Review Raffles – 'Students are issued with a Twitter review sheet for every book they take out of the LRC. They are asked to write a short review about the book, which is then posted to the author on our Twitter page @stwLRC. Students receive a raffle ticket for every review they write and are entered into a prize draw. If the author likes, retweets or even replies, I let the student know.'
- A 'What Should I Read Next?' Book Jar – 'All our fiction books have genre labels to help students choose their book easily. However, sometimes the students just do not know what they would like to read. I created a book jar that contains coloured paper slips. Each colour relates to a book genre and each slip contains a book recommendation. Students are invited to select a genre, then take out a piece of paper that matches the genre colour. Students excitedly run to find the book on the shelf and start reading. Student librarians update the jar on a regular basis.' (Suffield, 2019.)

Displays and stock promotion

- When starting your planning for displays and stock promotion, think about what the purpose of the display or promotion is, what impact and outcomes do you want it to achieve, and how will you measure these e.g. through student feedback, book loans, enquiries.
- Promotion of specific genres of stock can be done through displays, for example, romance with all pink book covers displayed or Shakespeare resources on Shakespeare's birthday.
- Top 10 tissue factor books – put the covers of a range of books on display and have tear shaped post-it notes available for students to stick next to the book cover with the number of tissues they think the book rates, from one to ten.
- Christmas advent calendar – put a book behind each window, recommended by a mix of staff and students; that person opens the window each day and talks about their chosen book.
- Wheel of 60 Carnegie winners – create a big wheel displaying the last 60 Carnegie Medal winners, each book displayed in a box alongside props from the story.
- When Castle Mead Academy in Leicester bought new Manga and graphic novels, instead of simply adding them to stock like normal, they

decided to make a feature of them and held a 'Manga Extravaganza' to boost the excitement and anticipation of the books. It was a roaring success.

■ Featuring books on the interface of your LMS can be very effective. Other ideas include: drawing students' attention to subject areas via carousels; showcasing lists; or just adding news items. Use display spinners to highlight genres such as horror before Halloween or romance near Valentine's Day or feature diverse authors during Pride Month and Black History Month.

■ Create a reading wall of titles and authors of children's favourite books.

■ For National Poetry Day, create a poet-tree with leaf templates on which children write lines from poems and staff write out their favourite childhood poem. Have them on the walls throughout the school as well as in the library.

■ Promote information books. Often, when people think about a reading culture in school and reading for pleasure, they will predominantly focus on promoting fiction stock and organising fiction-related reading activities. However, as the author of many successful information books, Andy Seed, says: 'So many children love reading factual books. A lot prefer them. I was one of those kids – I became a reader through them. Once I was a reader, I then developed a taste for fiction' (Seed, 2021). He also argues that 'Information books are an excellent way to engage children in reading for pleasure. Children will read what is enjoyable. They'll also read what they are into – so have lots of books which match interests' (Seed, 2020). Participating in the SLA (School Library Association) Information Book Award can provide an opportunity to reinforce the importance of information books and highlight the excellent range of books available.

■ Jenny Howe, Reading Engagement Co-ordinator at Queensbridge School, feels that 'to create a reading ethos in schools, lessons need to be linked to wider reading and the library. Working alongside a colleague in the English department, I decided it would be invaluable for our students to see more subject specific texts in the library. Subject teachers have volunteered as "Reading Champions" to make the non-fiction section even more relevant to their subjects. They have written bookshop style recommendations and we have placed these on the library shelves so students can see the link to subjects and wider reading. Students learn how important it is to broaden their reading horizons as part of their educational progress' (Howe, 2021).

Author events

An effective way of inspiring reading in school is to invite an author, illustrator, poet, or storyteller in to talk about their books and work with the students. This can be a rewarding experience for all involved, but it does need careful thought and planning to ensure everyone gets the best possible experience. The impact of a visiting author can be immense, as Eileen Armstrong, School Librarian at Cramlington Learning Village, highlights following a visit from author Curtis Jobling:

> This is one of the most successful visits we have ever had the pleasure of hosting. Students are still bringing me money for books every day and I'm having to collect more stock from the bookshop regularly to give out. It's generated such a buzz about books and reading. One of our teaching assistants also came to see me to tell me that one of our most severely autistic Year 7 students came along to Curtis' session. It was a huge thing for him to actually be in the Hub for the whole hour not knowing what would happen during the event. Afterwards his support assistant was amazed that he then spent lunchtime instigating conversations with other students about the trading cards, he never normally speaks much during the day and spends lunchtime on his own with his head in his hands. A day later he came to ask if he could have a copy of the book too. Transformative!

Zoe Rowley, Head Librarian at Wolverhampton Grammar School, who organises a regular programme of author visits to her school, says:

> Meeting an author, poet or illustrator can be inspirational for young people. It is often this experience which introduces children to new genres and starts them off on their journey to becoming an avid reader. When planning an event, use an organisation such as Authors Aloud UK to ensure that the author selected can deliver an appropriately inspiring workshop/presentation in your school. When planning the event, ensure that curriculum time has been allocated by the school and that a suitable location for the event is available. To ensure that the event is meaningful, children should be given time to read and discuss the opening extract of one of the author's books prior to the event. Competitions linked to the author's books can also be a great way to generate excitement linked to the author visit. Following the event, children should be given access to the author's books. By working with other school staff to get them to help with pre-preparation and follow up work, the school librarian can make the visit more effective.

Planning an author visit – what do you want to achieve?

Do you want to:

- improve literacy and/or visual literacy?
- put the fun back into reading for your students?
- widen children's reading horizons?
- get the school buzzing about reading?
- encourage children to write their own stories?
- encourage children to hear different people talking about books and reading?
- encourage the children to read more poetry and enjoy it?
- help the children understand more about the oral tradition and try telling stories for themselves?
- empower children to think of themselves as successful writers?
- enable the children/young people to meet the author whose books they are studying and be able to ask them questions?
- have a writing workshop to encourage the children's writing?
- treat the children to meeting an author whose books they are keen on and who they would love to meet?
- fit an author visit into a scheme of work?
- be able to tick the relevant National Curriculum box?
- gain positive publicity for the school?
- have this as part of a programme of events (for example, Book Week, PTA event)?

An author visit to your school can substantially contribute to all of these.

Organising the event – what do you need to think about?

- Once you know what you are aiming to achieve with your author visit, decide what sort of speaker you want – an author (of fiction or information books), a poet, an illustrator or a storyteller. Then begin to research which might work best for your school and inspire your students.
- If you are using an agency such as Authors Aloud UK, they will provide you with a list of suggested authors with a brief summary of what those authors do, based on the parameters of what you are looking for.
- Do you have the budget to cover the speaker's fee and expenses? Fees will vary from author to author. Some authors will offer half day visits, but usually within a geographical area that is local to where they live. It might be worth exploring sharing the cost of the visit with another local school, so that you each have the author for half a day. Also, consider

seeking sponsorship from a local firm or group, applying for a grant from a grant making body that supports this, or organising a sponsored event in school to raise funds (or ask parents or the PTA).

- Do you want the author to visit the school in person or through a virtual platform? Virtual author visits were developed during the COVID-19 pandemic as a method of still enabling students to have access to an author. While they can't offer the same experience as a visit to the school, they can offer different kinds of experiences and will continue as an alternative option.
- Do you want this visit to be a one-off visit? If you would like an author to work with your students over a longer period of time, then consider a Writer in Residence. A residency is the period of time a writer spends working with a particular organisation. Residencies can last weeks, months or even a year. Hosting a Writer in Residence can bring benefits to the school in terms of the creativity writers can inspire, the perspectives they can offer and the relationship that the writer can build with the students and staff.
- Who is your intended audience? Authors often specialise in writing books for a particular age group so make sure the author will be suitable for your intended age range.
- What do you want your author to deliver? Some writers offer a range of events, including readings, workshops and drama sessions, while others deliver a more traditional presentation (such as a talk with a Q&A session). Be creative in your thinking. Author, climber and explorer Matt Dickinson's expeditions to Everest, Antarctica and K2 have given him a wealth of fascinating real-life adventures to talk about with geography students, for instance, and pop-up and paper engineering author Robert Crowther delivers very effective sessions for art and graphic design students.
- How many sessions would you like from the author? Authors will on average do three or four sessions in a day. Some may do more, shorter sessions, others will do fewer. Many will do a large assembly-style presentation and then year group or classroom-based sessions – but be mindful of the author and be realistic in terms of how many sessions you ask for.
- Is the author available at the time you want them to visit? It's a good idea to plan well ahead – six to nine months is a good guideline – as authors can often get booked well ahead, especially around times of popular book celebrations, such as National Poetry Day and World Book Day.
- Are you going to provide the author's books for sale at the event? The opportunity to get a signed and dedicated copy of one of the author's

books can be a special experience for the students. Authors enjoy the chance to sign books and talk to students at the end of their events, so it is always good to offer this. Ask your local bookshop or supplier if they will provide you with copies on a sale-or-return basis. (If you are booking through an agency, they can often help you link with a bookseller if you don't already have one.) Some booksellers will be willing to give a discount on the price per copy and come to the school to do the selling for you. It is always worth asking.

Finding and booking your author

- Use an agency such as: Authors Aloud UK (www.authorsalouduk.co.uk); Apples and Snakes (for poets) (https://applesandsnakes.org); Contact an Author (https://contactanauthor.co.uk); or Speaking of Books (www.speakingofbooks.co.uk). An agency will take a lot of the hard work of organising the event with the author away from you, so that you can focus on the in-school organisation.
- Contact the publisher of the author you are interested in booking.
- Booksellers may organise an author event for their schools, so it is worth checking with your local bookshop.
- Reach out to an author via social media – they can then let you know what the best way is of booking them. Many will direct you to their bookings agency or publisher, but some may be happy to liaise with you directly.

Publisher tours and events for authors

Some publishers will organise a tour, event or book launch for some of their authors on publication of a new book. The publisher will set the criteria for the tour events that a host school will need to meet. This will include the audience size, audience age range and whether it needs to be a multi-school event with the host school inviting other local schools to join in. The publisher will always stipulate that books by the author should be available for sale on the day and/or through pre-orders. They will have schools that they work with regularly, but you may consider contacting a publisher to ask if any of their authors are going to be touring and visiting schools.

Authors Aloud UK often organise tours and events for authors on behalf of the publisher. They are always looking for new schools who can meet the criteria and are interested in hosting and organising a visit. Author opportunities are usually advertised through networks such as SLN (School Librarians Network) and CILIP SLG, as well as directly to schools who have previously hosted a tour visit or expressed an interest in doing so. Tour events are free to the school. It is possible to express your interest in being considered as a tour school by completing the form on the Tour tab of the website: https://authorsalouduk.co.uk/tours.

Patron of Reading

You may wish to look at developing a longer, more in-depth relationship with an author, in which case the Patron of Reading scheme (https://patronofreading.co.uk) could be what you are looking for. A school can choose a Patron of Reading and develop a relationship with them over time. The patron will work with the school to help cultivate, promote, support and encourage a reading for pleasure culture and a reading rich environment in the school.

Five top tips for a successful author visit

1 If possible, allow the students to be familiar with the author's books before the visit. Have displays in the library, make sure books are available to borrow from the library or, if you are inviting another school in, make sure the teacher has encouraged their students to read some of the books.
2 Make sure that school staff know when the author is coming and have someone who can take the reins if, for instance, you are ill on the day.
3 Ensure the author is welcomed to the school, introduced at each of their sessions, looked after throughout the visit and provided with appropriate refreshments.
4 Find out in advance what equipment and materials the author will need and make sure they are available. Also make sure that any required IT works. The venue needs to be appropriate for the event taking place, with external noise kept to a minimum and no constant stream of people wandering in and out, potentially disrupting the event.
5 HAVE FUN AND ENJOY!

Five top tips for a successful virtual author visit

1 If possible, allow the students to be familiar with the author's books before the visit. Have displays in the library, make sure books are available for children to borrow from the library.
2 Make sure your IT staff can handle a virtual visit effectively, that the author knows what platform it is going to be hosted on and what they

need to do to access it on the day. Check the author has received the link and always do a tech check with them before the event begins, to make sure all is working well. Leave enough time to put things right before the event is due to start. Don't forget to introduce the author before they begin the session and thank them at the end.

3 Try to enable the author to see the students they are talking to, to improve their interaction. If this isn't possible because you have more than one school taking part and for safeguarding reasons it needs to be done as a webinar, then make sure you stay on screen to respond to what they are saying.

4 Plan how you want the students to interact with the author and ask questions. Will you let them ask questions live on screen or via the chat or the Q & A facility?

5 HAVE FUN AND ENJOY!

The Society of Authors has a useful guide for schools organising an author visit: https://societyofauthors.org/SOA/MediaLibrary/SOAWebsite/Guides/A-Guide-for-Schools-Organising-an-Author-Visit.pdf.

The rights of the reader

We all know the benefits of reading and the positive impact it has on us in terms of mental health and wellbeing, skills and comprehension, concentration and focus, and pleasure and learning. Because of this, we are passionate in trying to encourage students and other staff to read for pleasure. However, we do need to remember that readers have rights, the reading experience will be different for each reader and there will always be non-readers. In his book, *The Rights of the Reader*, Daniel Pennac outlines what those rights are. These were produced as a poster illustrated by Quentin Blake (Pennac and Blake, 2006):

1 The right not to read.
2 The right to skip.
3 The right not to finish a book.
4 The right to read it again.
5 The right to read anything.
6 The right to mistake a book for real life.
7 The right to read anywhere.
8 The right to dip in.
9 The right to read aloud.
10 The right to be quiet.

Pennac goes on to say, '10 rights, 1 warning – Don't make fun of people who don't read – or they never will!' (Pennac and Blake, 2006). The challenge for the school librarian is to find ways to enthuse and hopefully convert those non-readers without them feeling pressure to read in an expected way and to let them read in their own way if they do begin to read.

Valerie Dewhurst, Head of Library at Queen Elizabeth's Grammar School in Blackburn, sums this up:

> It doesn't matter how … It really doesn't matter how a book is read – print or digital. It really does not matter where it is read – the school library, school bus, quiet reading corner in a classroom, at home. What matters is that reading is happening and being enjoyed. Using mobile devices and iPads to access eBooks is without doubt something we should be promoting if this helps us to rekindle, restore, or resurrect reading habits.
>
> (Dewhurst, 2021)

Funding sources

While many of your ideas for activities and events can often be done at no cost or within available school resources, there may be times when you want to look for additional funding support. There are several publications and websites that offer opportunities to look for grant making bodies that will support school activities, such as: the Directory of Grant Making Trusts, a printed book produced annually; Grants for Schools (www.grants4schools. info); and Grants Online (www.grantsonline.org.uk). Most of them will require a subscription to access the information. If you are looking for potential funding opportunities, it is worth checking whether your school or local authority already subscribes to one of these that you could have access to.

The following are grant making organisations that will consider and support applications from schools and school libraries:

- Give a Book (http://giveabook.org.uk)
- Siobhan Dowd Trust (http://siobhandowdtrust.com)
- Foyle Foundation (www.foylefoundation.org.uk/how-to-apply/state-schools.php)
- Paul Hamlyn Foundation (www.phf.org.uk).

Working with other school staff

A librarian working on their own will only be able to achieve so much. For a reading rich environment to be developed and embedded within the school culture, it needs to be owned and supported by the Headteacher and all staff across the school. It is all about communication and enthusiasm, so let others know what the school library is doing, what you are trying to achieve and what the impact is for the school and the students. Encourage them to see that these are ongoing whole school projects. Work on engaging the Head and the SLT as library champions and remember that this is a long-term strategy for the school, not just for a defined timeframe such as World Book Day, even if you also want their support for specific initiatives.

Let teaching staff see that the librarian is not a threat but a potential ally, working on similar priorities but from a slightly different angle (that is, not literacy in the sense of decoding, but in the widest sense of developing curiosity, excitement, lifelong learning and awareness, and of opening the doors of aspiration). Ask the literacy co-ordinator, the Head of English and other relevant staff how they feel the library could support what they are trying to achieve. Explore ways to work with individual class teachers in primary schools or subject leads in secondary schools. You may find that not all staff will want to engage, so initially concentrate on the keen ones. When others see the success and impact of working with you, it may prompt them to come on board for a future initiative. There are many strategies that you can employ including:

- Go to Head of Department meetings, discuss your ideas for the library with them and seek their views on how the library can support their teaching. Offer to hold departmental meetings in the library and show teachers the books in their subject areas. This can work well as they will then hopefully tell their students to visit and borrow the resources.
- Ask staff what they think about books, what their book needs are and try to meet those needs. If you want to try to change the approaches of the Head, SLT or specific teachers, perhaps suggest a project and demonstrate from research why it could be good for the school. Consider taking part in projects run by organisations such as the Reading Agency, National Literacy Trust and Read for Good as they will often include evaluation and impact assessments that you can use to support a case for future involvement.
- The library should be included in schemes of work (SoW) for all departments. Initially, a good way to begin this work is to plan a research skills session to teach young people basic information literacy skills. The CILIP Information Literacy Group has resources that can

assist in the planning of such sessions (https://infolit.org.uk/information-literacy-group/school-resource-sheets). More information on this is covered in Chapter 5: Information and Digital Literacy. By selecting one department to initially deliver this to, teachers can begin to see the success of such work as students improve the quality of their research-based work. Delivering a staff training session on how the library can support reading and research will also ensure good partnerships between the school librarian and all departments. By supporting students in the development of research and literacy skills, the library will become an integral component in academic success.

- Deliver a whole school INSET session. Send a questionnaire to staff asking what they want from the library. Ask for reading lists and curriculum information so that you can bring the library to them.
- Getting other staff involved by asking them to take responsibility for part or all of a project can be very effective. For example, get them involved in organising events, picking books for book awards or joining book group meetings.
- Get parents, families and the community involved in what you are planning and delivering and ask them to help.
- Empower students to get involved. Recruit and use pupil library assistants to promote reading and the library. By offering young people the opportunity to become pupil library assistants you will be allowing them to develop confidence and communication skills in a position of responsibility. Inviting students of all ages to apply for this position by writing an expression of interest letter allows them to begin embarking on this form of work experience. Pupil library assistants can become ambassadors for reading across the school by promoting a book of the week, running outdoor libraries, keeping displays up to date and taking new stock suggestions from their peers. They can become a valuable source of support for the school librarian.

Schools Library Services

An effective, value for money source of support for schools and school librarians in helping create a reading rich environment is your local Schools Library Service. SLSs can provide a school with access to a cost-effective range of resources, advice, guidance, training and support. They are run by experienced, qualified librarians who have both a good knowledge of children's literature and of the curriculum and resources to support it. Although the way each service operates will vary from authority to authority, SLSs offer a range of services to subscribers that can include:

- project or topic collection loans
- class reading sets
- annual book loans
- school visits and workshops
- story sack loans
- online resources and lending platforms
- book purchase schemes
- artefact boxes and costume loans
- support for library management systems
- cataloguing expertise
- advice on library stock development and maintenance
- library design, redesign, auditing and editing packages
- professional library advice and guidance
- policy and development planning
- author events
- training for school staff
- reading group support
- support for schools participating in national awards and initiatives
- organisation and delivery of local book awards
- networking opportunities for school library staff
- support for reading activities
- information literacy lessons – advice, training and delivery.

Examples of the range of services that may be available are demonstrated by the following Schools Library Services:

- Coventry Schools Library and Resource Service (www.coventry.gov.uk/sls)
- Creative Learning Services, Leicestershire (www.creativelearningservices.org.uk)
- Redbridge Schools Library Service (www.redbridge.gov.uk/libraries/schools-library-service)
- Tower Hamlets Schools Library Service (www.towerhamlets-sls.org.uk).

Although not all authorities have a Schools Library Service, some will offer services to schools outside their local area. In addition, the Association of Senior Children's and Education Librarians (ASCEL), working in partnership with Schools Library Services, have established SLS UK. This consists of a collective of Schools Library Services covering the length and breadth of the UK and offering subscriptions, consultancy and librarian services for schools. Run by experienced qualified librarians, their mission is to be a catalyst for learning by providing teachers and schools with the ideas, research and resources they need to deliver positive outcomes for students.

For further information, see:

- SLS UK (https://sls-uk.org)
- Association of Senior Children's and Education Librarians (https://ascel.org.uk/school-library-services)
- School Library Association (www.sla.org.uk/school-library-services).

Conclusion

When Cressida Cowell became the 11th Children's Laureate, she wanted to champion children's books, get even more children reading and for every child to read for fun and get something out of books. From this she developed her Children's Laureate Charter, which states that every child has the right to:

1   Read for the joy of it.
2   Access new books in schools, libraries and bookshops.
3   Have advice from a trained librarian or bookseller.
4   Own their own book.
5   See themselves reflected in a book.
6   Be read aloud to.
7   Have some choice in what they read.
8   Be creative for at least 15 minutes a week.
9   See an author event at least once.
10   Have a planet to read on.

Cressida's Charter can be downloaded and printed off here: https://cdn.booktrust.org.uk/globalassets/resources/childrens-laureate/2019-21/cressida_waterstones_charter_a3_2022.pdf.

If you are a new school librarian starting out on your journey to creating a rich reading culture and environment in the library and school in which you are working and are hoping to inspire students to read for pleasure and learning, perhaps one of the first questions to ask yourself is: What is my school doing to fulfil these rights and what can I as the school librarian do to help?

Action points

1 Investigate the national book initiatives section of this chapter and see what opportunities each offers.
2 Choose one national book initiative and plan how to get your school involved in it.
3 Choose one suggested activity in the practical ideas for creating a reading rich environment section and plan how and when you could introduce it to your school.
4 Draw up a plan for an author visit to your school.
5 Do an online search for funding for one reading-related activity for your school and plan an application for it.
6 Read at least one of the reference sources cited in this chapter.
7 Explore two of the websites cited in this chapter.
8 Print off the Children's Laureate and the Rights of the Reader Charters and display them in the library.

Further reading

Clements, J. (2017) *Building an Outstanding Reading School*, https://cdn.oxfordowl.co.uk/2017/04/21/10/51/51/265/bp_osi_buildingoutstanding.pdf.
Court, J. (ed.) (2011) *Read to Succeed*, Facet Publishing.
Pennac, D. (2006) *The Rights of the Reader*, Walker Books.
Quigley, A. (2020) *Closing the Reading Gap*, Routledge.

5

Information Literacy and Digital Literacy

Sarah Pavey

Introduction

This chapter considers the theory and practicalities of teaching information and digital literacy. We learn about the different formal models we might use and how to plan and deliver lessons through collaboration with subject teachers.

The National Literacy Trust defines literacy as 'the ability to read, write, speak and listen in a way that lets us communicate effectively and make sense of the world' (2021). Within a school, this is the type of literacy that is assessed in an inspection and there may be a specific committee dedicated to improving these learning goals. Many other more specific literacies are now referred to within education and two of importance to school librarianship are information literacy and digital literacy. Essentially, these terms relate to the understanding of the use of information in all its forms and similarly for digital products. However, the use of this terminology is not always consistent. It is open to interpretation. For this reason, some organisations have tried to define the terms more explicitly.

Defining digital literacy

Many people mistake digital literacy for the ability to use basic computer skills in relation to hardware, software and online resources, and applying these in context. Others regard digital literacy as the ability to operate digital technology and related resources in a safe and secure way. Whilst e-safety and security are essential aspects of digital literacy, this is far from the whole picture. Digital literacy is about being able to operate in the digital world in its widest sense and this embraces a range of skills that are needed for life.

The American Library Association's Digital Literacy Task Force offers this definition:

> Digital literacy is the ability to use information and communication technologies to find, evaluate, create, and communicate information, requiring both cognitive and technical skills.
>
> (ALA, 2013)

Jisc suggests it is 'the capabilities which fit someone for living, learning and working in a digital society' (2018). In the UK, the Jisc Model Seven Elements of Digital Literacy (2018) is the most recognised by higher education. It incorporates:

- media literacy
- communications and collaboration
- career and identity management
- ICT literacy
- learning skills
- digital scholarship
- information literacy.

Unfortunately, within the National Curriculum for England and Wales (DfE, 2021b), the extent of digital literacy instruction is very much limited to the use of information technology tools and safeguarding. Other schools in countries adopting a more inquiry-based learning approach will accept a wider definition.

Defining information literacy

Information literacy was defined as a universal human right by UNESCO as part of the Alexandria Proclamation (2006). But what does the term mean in practice? Again, we find the context of use confusing. In 2018, CILIP's Information Literacy Group (ILG) produced a new definition that encompassed the ways in which information use and understanding had changed since the UNESCO declaration.

The ILG definition states that:

> Information literacy is the ability to think critically and make balanced judgements about any information we find and use. It empowers us as citizens to reach and express informed views and to engage fully with society.
>
> (CILIP ILG, 2018, 3)

How information literacy can be understood within different contexts of everyday life, citizenship, health, the workplace and education is underpinned by examples within the ILG document.

When working with terminology that is open to interpretation, it can be difficult for us to engage with teachers and senior leaders so that they understand the importance of the student competencies we are trying to support by offering opportunities for practice. This means that the degree to which we may be involved in the teaching of digital literacy and information literacy will depend upon how the curriculum is delivered in individual schools. If we wish to pursue this cross-curricular approach to lifelong learning skills, we will need to be certain this ambition fits with the wider mission statement of the school.

Models for teaching information and digital literacy

If we want to teach information and digital literacy skills, we may find it useful to have a robust framework underpinned by academic research to suggest to our line managers. However, this is not prescribed or even essential. We may discover another methodology that works more effectively in our own school. First, we need to decide on the type of information literacy model we wish to use. Essentially, there are three different approaches we can consider:

- search and use: these models promote higher level thinking and decision taking
- information inquiry: these models encourage students to reflect and revise to aid the synthesis and embedding of information that is found
- discipline specific: these models are designed for use with specific curriculum subjects that may require a specialised approach to information handling.

Within each of these model groups, there is a wealth of products to choose from and many are freely available. It is worth investigating a few to gain an understanding of the aims and competencies they seek to impart. Table 5.1 on the next page summarises choices that are popular in schools worldwide.

A list of references to these models is given in Appendix 4. In the UK, the most prevalent are BIG 6 (and Super 3), PLUS, ISP and, more recently, FOSIL, which is based on Stripling's Empire State Information Fluency Continuum (ESIFC). Here, we can see how formal models might look in practice.

Firstly, we will consider a 'search and use' approach from a secondary school.

Table 5.1 *Selection of information literacy models used by schools worldwide*

Search and use	Inquiry based	Discipline specific
5As (Macdonald, Dosaj & Jukes) BAT (younger students – simplified PSU) (Nesset) BIG 6 (Eisenberg & Berkowitz) FLIP IT (Yucht) I-Learn (Neuman et al.) Irvings (Irving) Information Search Process (ISP) (Kuhlthau) PLUS (Herring) PSU (Nesset) REACTS (Stripling & Pitts) Simple Four (Alewine) Super 3 (younger students – simplified BIG 6)	8Ws (Lamb) Alberta Dimensions of Inquiry (INFOhio) Empire State Information Fluency Continuum (ESIFC) (Stripling) FOSIL (Toerien) (UK adapted version of ESIFC) Imposed Query (Gross) Inquiry Cycle (Gourley) I-Search (Macrorie) Noodle Tools (Abilock) Pathways to Knowledge (Pappas & Tepe) Pre-search (Rankin) Research Cycle (McKenzie) WebQuests (Dodge)	5E Inquiry Model (Bybee) Humanities Model of Inquiry (Bateman) Problem Based Learning (McMaster) Science Technology Society (STS) Inquiry Model (Joyce & Weil) Scientific Method Suchman Inquiry Model Zoom-In Inquiry

We used the Big 6 model for history projects for KS3 (11–13-year-olds). Using a model helps prevent the students just going to Google and copying/pasting what they find. It gives them the reason to be selective and critical of the resources they find before using them. There are six steps. First, they define the task and we let them brainstorm. Secondly, they look at what types of sources they might use and we introduce them to the CRAAP test and refer back to the brainstorm to think about keywords. Thirdly, they need to decide how they are going to find the information. Fourthly, when they have to record the information they find, we show them about referencing and making a bibliography. Next, we consider note-taking and how to construct their presentation. For the final step six of evaluation, we have a mark rubric and introduce peer assessment. It all works very well and they seem to become much more engaged with the topics.

Let us now look at an information inquiry-based model. For this to be effective in practice, the subject needs to be investigative either through experimentation or because divided opinion about the topic exists. The research model involves more than simply finding an answer, evaluating the source and communicating what you have found to others.

The students in Year 9 (12–13-year-olds) were given a topic to investigate asking why finding a smallpox cure had been so important in England, as part of a science class on infectious diseases. We used the FOSIL model as the scaffold for their independent learning project. They began with 'Connect' and considered why this might be an important question to answer. They used the 'Wonder' thread to think about what questions they would need to ask and how to find the answers. 'Investigate' introduced them to searching for resources to answer the questions and they learned about note taking, reference information and quotations. Moving to 'Construct', they pieced together the information they had gathered in a logical order and thought about the message they were conveying through their presentation. 'Express' allowed them to refine and add personal reflection to their final production. 'Reflect' was completed last and here they considered why the results of the research were an important contribution to history more generally. It certainly gave them freedom to investigate for themselves in a different way to just gathering random facts. They had to reflect on the purpose of the information and tell the story.

When working with younger students or those with special needs, we may need to adapt the research process and just consider the basic requirements. Good learning outcomes can be achieved using one of the simpler models as the next example shows.

The Year 4 (8–9-year-olds) were conducting a project on the Romans. We decided to use the BAT (Beginning, Acting, Telling) model of information literacy to help them understand the research skills they needed. The good thing about this model is it is adaptable and can include more complex elements for the more able students. 'Beginning' involves thinking about the topic and reading and discussing what is to be investigated. 'Acting' concerns sorting out the vocabulary that will be needed, gathering the information and deciding what to use. 'Telling' is about preparing what has been found and selected for the presentation. They loved the idea of bats and everyone made their plan for research on a bat-shaped template, which we then displayed alongside the posters they produced.

Similarly, there are also models for digital literacy. Three that are commonly used are:

- Digital Literacy Across the Curriculum (Hague and Peyton, 2010)
- New Media Literacies (Jenkins, 2006)
- Eight Essential Elements of Digital Literacy (Belshaw, 2014).

References to these models can be found in Appendix 5.

Digital literacy models focus on the use of technology to help with research and understanding of topics. These three exemplar models all differ in their learning objectives.

Hague and Peyton consider digital literacy in terms of the key skills students need to develop. By focusing on the nature of the skill, the model helps students develop transferable skills. They argue that only then can consideration be given to the use of technology. The Hague and Peyton model seeks to make the embedding of skills across the curriculum in different subjects more meaningful.

The Jenkins model suggests that schools need to devote more time to cultural competencies and social skills embracing the collaboration, networking and deep learning that digital technologies might support. Using this model involves focusing on specific media, looking at cultural exchange and the social skills that can be supported by digital technology.

Belshaw's eight essential elements, or 8Cs, identify the skills an individual needs to gain to become digitally literate. These areas for consideration are: cultural; cognitive; constructive; communicative; confidence; creative; critical; and civic.

There is an overlap between the information literacy and digital literacy models and it is possible that we might choose elements of both and blend them together.

The challenge with using a model, whether for information literacy or digital literacy, is that it assumes a student is working independently. This may not be the case, particularly within an exam-based curriculum. Galley (2017), although in a primary school context, suggests that using an 'imposed query' model might be more relevant to an English curriculum. Models can also place restrictions on how information and digital literacy might be delivered in practice. Many models assume a linear or cyclical approach when in fact research is often a 'messy' process. So, we might decide just to use elements of a model and not necessarily stick with a strict order. A series of 'Research Smarter' leaflets, detailing approaches to different components of the research process, has been developed by the Information Literacy Group (ILG) and these can be downloaded for free from their website: https://infolit.org.uk/information-literacy-group/school-resource-sheets.

Let's consider now how we might teach information and digital literacy in practice.

Information and digital literacy lessons – opportunities, location and planning

The opportunities to teach information and digital literacy will vary between schools. For some of us, it may be a dedicated set of library lessons; others may deliver skills through the taught requirements for the Extended Project Qualification (EPQ) or other project-based work. However, for many of us it will be a matter of spotting opportunities and coaxing teaching staff on board in an ad hoc manner. In England and Wales, the National Curriculum and exam board syllabi rarely require formal teaching of information and digital literacy aside from being a small part of some subjects, such as Citizenship, Computing and Media Studies. So, what do we do?

It is beneficial to study the National Curriculum and exam board criteria in depth. This can help us to identify areas where an inquiry approach to learning might be possible. Next, we can approach subject teachers and invite them to collaborate with us in the lesson delivery. Not all teachers will feel able to accept our offer, but we should seek out the staff who want to work with us and use the learning outcomes from these lessons to persuade others.

True collaborative practice happens when there is joint planning and agreement on the learning objectives of the lesson. Teachers are experts in developing formal lesson plans and we should allow ourselves to be guided by them. However, we are the information experts and can contribute to provision of resources and instruction about the use of these resources. By using parts or the whole of an information literacy model, we can use the academic language to which a teacher can relate.

Having devised a plan for the lesson, we need to think about where it will take place. Pavey (2005) considered the pros and cons of delivering lessons in the library and the classroom and concluded that beginning with classroom delivery, followed by research in the library, yielded positive outcomes. By using this approach, the formal setting of the classroom with the teacher sets a familiar environment for learning for the students. This enables the librarian to ensure the students understand how they will undertake their research work before they move to the more informal setting of the library. It also underpins that the teacher sets the research learning objectives and assessment structure, but the librarian can advise on resources and how they might be used. Being involved in the awarding of some marks reaps rewards too, as students then perceive us as integral to the learning process.

It could be that we are not able to collaborate and have been directed to deliver a set of discrete lessons on information and digital literacy rather than to embed these competencies within a subject area. Here, to maximise the chance of transferring skills, it is useful to relate what we teach to subjects in the curriculum that the students may be studying. Our setting will be our library, but it is advisable – if space allows – to ensure there is a classroom type area or at least a formal atmosphere when delivering the lesson plan. Lesson planning is a necessary skill and we can get ideas by watching and talking to teaching staff. There are also websites where you can download lesson plan templates. By using these, we can demonstrate to our line managers that we understand about learning objectives and outcomes and the wider educational benefit of what we teach.

Teaching elements of information and digital literacy

A lesson plan can help us define objectives and set out the nature of the elements we will teach, but how can we deliver our message in a meaningful way and ensure learning has taken place? Very few librarians in the UK are dual qualified as teachers and the temptation is just to deliver a lecture using slides. We need to be mindful that students are more familiar with an interactive approach and so we may need to be more creative. This is a challenge! Teaching referencing and bibliography creation hardly seems exciting. Let us look at some ideas.

Planning research

The structure of research will to some extent be dictated by the subject and purpose of the work. A scientific experiment and report will be different in approach to a long essay for a humanities subject. Other research work will be discursive and based upon evaluating opinion rather than fact. Nonetheless, most information literacy models will advocate beginning with a 'brainstorming' session to see what is already known and what the scope of the work will be. One method is to use a 'mind map' as a structure, but we could also make use of the many collaborative apps that are available such as Jamboard   (https://support.google.com/jamboard/answer/7424836?hl=en), Post-it Plus (www.3m.co.uk/3M/en_GB/post-it-notes/ideas/app) or Nearpod (https://nearpod.com).

The research with Year 12 students (16–17-year-olds) studying English focused on the question 'Should a novel challenge or entertain the reader?' The class was divided in two and each tasked to come up with questions to support the viewpoint they were to argue from. They wrote the questions on square sticky notes and then photographed them with the app Post-it Plus and uploaded them to a collaborative board. The whole class discussion showed the board and the notes could be moved. Together a structure for the investigation was developed that the whole class could follow using the questions as a guide.

  Year 7 (11–12-year-olds) were researching elements for science. There were a number of facts that they had to gather that had been chosen by their subject teacher. Together we planned a template that could be filled in for the element they had been given. The class discussion then considered where the information might be found. In pairs, the students were given a couple of books, articles or websites selected by the librarian and the students had to decide whether the sources would be useful. They reported back to the class their views. This also enabled the librarian to see what the students needed and to adapt the resources offered.

Searching and finding information

From the planning and brainstorming session, students can begin to get a sense of the vocabulary they might need for effective searching. However, the temptation is just to put the title of the research into Google, find the Wikipedia reference and copy it without thought. Students are so used to looking for information online, they have little sense of hierarchy, so teaching them to use an index works well as a starter exercise. Twenge, Campbell and Sherman (2019) noted that vocabulary levels have significantly dropped over the last few decades. In the following scenarios, we see practical examples that address this concern and invite our students to learn more about the effective use of keywords.

The Year 8 students (12–13-year-olds) were divided into pairs and each was given a dictionary. They chose a starting word for their research project and wrote that in the centre of a large piece of paper. One student looked up the word in the dictionary and read out all the other words associated with it in the entry. The second student wrote these words down and drew connecting lines from the original word. The second student then chose one of the new words and looked that up in the dictionary and the other student recorded the information. The game continued until all possibilities had been added and then the students highlighted the ten best words to use for a keyword search.

To help students understand about using keywords, one student becomes the internet and sits with their back to the screen. A picture is projected onto the screen with a keyword written underneath. The rest of the class offer alternative words so that the 'internet student' can try and guess what word is written on the screen. The alternatives are written down so they can all be seen on a flipchart. The game progresses from a simple word to two words that need to be searched separately to be understood, for example, 'red car', then to a subjective word, such as 'success', and finally to a word that might have multiple meanings, such as 'resistance'. This gives students a feel for the complexity of an internet search and the potential pitfalls.

Another lesson that we might plan is showing our students where to look for information. We can discuss with them the differences between primary, secondary and tertiary resources using a quiz style approach and by using scenarios related to their research methodology.

For example, Abi is investigating the impact of the planting of trees in her local community for her EPQ. What kind of resource would she use for the following?

1 Background information on the benefits of tree planting.
2 Finding out about how much planting had taken place in her area over the last five years.
3 Discovering the attitudes of local people to the new woodland areas.

This method would also work with younger children, asking:

■ What resource do you use to look up the meaning of a word?

- What resource do you use to find out about a recent event?
- What resource do you use to read a story about something?

It is important that we show students the full range of media options available to them when looking for information and to illustrate that taking extracts and facts from a variety of sources protects to some extent against bias and misconception. It is an easy trap just to lecture students about all the information resources you have, but many will not be listening to what you say. It is difficult for students to understand the purpose of the knowledge you are imparting if they do not have the practical experience to interpret its meaning. Hence, it is best practice for us to devise lessons where students can participate and either follow instructions on use or better still experiment and find out for themselves. A short plenary at the end of the lesson will confirm what has been learned and any gaps can be identified and filled by us as facilitators.

Students were given a list of the subscription and free databases that the library management system (LMS) had as links. In pairs, the class were given a specific database to work with and asked to use keywords associated with the topic of renewable energy to find information. The librarian and science teacher offered help and guidance when it was requested. At the end of the lesson, students reported back on what they had found and commented on how easy the database had been to use, its pros and cons and suitability for the topic. The librarian felt that the students had gained more information about the databases and by gaining practical experience felt more confident in their own ability to use them.

Selecting and recording information

Sifting through the many sources of information takes time and some students may find the process overwhelming. Research work often presents as a novel scenario as most students are more familiar with extracting specified information from a single source and presenting their findings immediately. As librarians, we can explain that inquiry work takes time and as a first step it is useful to gather as much relevant information as possible so that we become familiar and immersed in the topic. This repetition aids memory retention. Nonetheless, students may find it difficult to work with non-fiction texts and not understand how to discern which information they might need for their work.

Information can be presented in many different forms, all of which require specific reading techniques. We might choose to develop a lesson to allow students to practise these skills:

Tables were set up, each with five books requiring a different type of reading:

■ finding a word in an index
■ finding a word in the contents page
■ finding information from a diagram
■ skimming for information in a book with no index or contents page
■ making your own subjective decision about information to use.

On top of the pile of books was a different set of questions for each table that tested the ability of students to find information in the five different ways. For example, the diagram information might be tested in a book of symbols or a dictionary showing a labelled diagram. Making a choice might be a book on making a cake for a party and asking them to choose the one they like best.

A maximum of ten minutes was given for each table. A plenary at the end discussed what skills were needed to find the information? What was easiest and what was most challenging? Did it get easier with practice?

When the intrinsic motivation of inquiry work kicks in, we find ourselves in a state defined as 'flow' (Nakamura, Dwight and Shankland, 2019). This is when we are so absorbed in our actions that we cannot think of anything else. Unfortunately, for many students this also means they may forget to record the source of their information. While teachers may have drilled their students in note-taking for printed texts, they do not always transfer this skill to other media. It is important for us to show students the value of recording information and why this is necessary, as well as practical techniques for information discovery. In the next example, we see an information literacy lesson addressing this learning objective.

The librarian showed a slide on the screen with a statistical graph about use of social media by age to the class. No explanation was given, the class were just asked to read it, but they also had paper given to them. The librarian then removed the slide and asked the class to take a sheet of paper and write a heading – 'The effect of age on social media use' – and to write sentences based on what they had seen on the slide. The librarian observed who had been taking notes and called on selected students to read out what they had composed. Most students had not taken notes, struggled to remember, made up facts or confessed they should have written something down. A debate then ensued on the value of note-taking.

Interestingly, this librarian repeated the exercise in the same lesson using a video and again most students fell into the same trap! Transfer of skills is a hard concept and constant repetition in different circumstances yields better results. We are giving our students practical experiences they can draw upon when faced with similar scenarios.

Living in a world of smart devices drives recording information beyond the traditional concept of physical note-taking using pen and paper. Students can now be shown how to use the camera and microphone on their phones or tablets to take pictures or videos of experiments and resources they use or simply to use voice to text technology to extract short notes for later use. A plethora of specialist apps exists to aid this process, which can be discovered through the various app stores or by using a generic app search engine such as AppCrawlr (http://appcrawlr.com). Examples include: Evernote (https://evernote.com); OneNote (www.onenote.com); Notion (www.notion.so); and Google Keep (www.google.com/keep). Some, such as Penultimate (https://help.evernote.com/hc/en-us/articles/209122017-Penultimate-Quick-Start-Guide), Notability (https://notability.com) and Squid (www.squidnotes.com), allow students to add handwriting annotations. The Inkflow app (www.qrayon.com/ home/inkflow) is specifically about visual notes.

Nonetheless, despite all this wonderful technology, it is useful for students to learn to take notes in a more traditional way too. Here, we can build upon the techniques we may have used in lessons about searching for information and the importance of keywords. Many teachers use 'cloze' activities to achieve this. These are sheets of texts with missing words and the student must select from a list which word would be most appropriate in each space. This type of exercise can also be used in other ways to help with the recording of information.

The students were each given a photocopy of an article. They were asked to cut out the words or short sentences that would be useful for writing the article in their own words. They then threw away what they had not used and tried to write the sense of the piece, sticking words they had found on the paper and writing their own text around the words. In a discussion after completion, we talked about how easy the piece had been to write, whether they had chosen the right words, what went wrong and what went well. They then reflected on how they might do this again – maybe differently.

It is also important for us to explain to students how they should record information about the sources they use to compile a bibliography. We will consider academic honesty in more depth later, but when gathering information, it is necessary for students to understand the components they need to note. Knowing that the function of referencing is to allow other readers to retrace the elements that led to your conclusions and opinions, rather than just assuming this information is simply to show you did not copy your work from someone else, is fundamental. Many databases allow students to copy a citation format from sources they use and perhaps your LMS has this functionality too. Again, there are apps that allow students to scan the ISBN barcode of a book and produce a citation in several formats, which can be saved or e-mailed. These include Citationsy, Easy Referencing and AlleyDog. Alternatively, students can use the referencing tab in a Word programme to create references too.

Evaluating the information

We might also choose to plan information literacy lessons around the concept of evaluating the credibility of the information. The rise in concern about 'fake news', misinformation, disinformation and malinformation may trigger teachers to contact us and ask for help in explaining this to students. Unfortunately, the curriculum in England and Wales treats this skill as spotting false information, rather than understanding why the information has been published, so it may be that what we see as the learning objective and what the teacher requires differ.

Another communication issue that might arise with students is that the use of the word 'evaluate' in the curriculum of England and Wales is not what we are given to understand. Here, it means consider your own work and think about how well you have achieved the objectives of the lesson. Getting students and teaching staff to appreciate the need to consider the purpose of the literature and to apply critical literacy criteria can be difficult to achieve.

Again, there are models we can use in our teaching, such as the descriptively named CRAAP test (Blakeslee, 2004). This is an acronym for Currency, Relevance, Authority, Accuracy and Purpose. Many university websites include a guide to its use, often with video content too. Other models that focus on the source information include RADAR (Rationale, Authority, Date, Accuracy, Relevance) (Mandalios, 2013) and 5Ws 1H (Who? What? When? Where? Why? How?) (Radom and Gammons, 2014). SIFT: The Four Moves (Caulfield, 2017) takes a slightly different approach by looking at the context of the information. Here, the letters represent: Stop (slow down and think about the information), Investigate, Find and Trace. All these approaches provide a strong scaffold on which to plan our lessons. References to these models are in Appendix 6.

Critical literacy is another aspect of information evaluation that we can help students understand. If we assume that most text information is created by humans, then we accept that the author will choose what to include and what to leave out. Choices are made about the subjects and people that are represented in the written piece. Readers, too, will have different experiences and knowledge and may therefore interpret texts in different ways. Overall, we can see how an article can influence our actions and our use of it in a piece of research. Deeper understanding of how information is constructed, its 'architecture', can help us to evaluate the content. In the next example we see how this might be made more explicit to students.

The students were given an unusual object. They handed it around the class and everyone had to ask a question about it, such as: What was it made from? What was its value? How old was it? The librarian wrote the questions on the board. Next, for each question, the students thought about who would need to know the answer and for what purpose. There was then discussion about how the write-up about the object would differ according to the intended audience. The object was then substituted by a research article and the same process followed. This gave the students a greater sense of the rationale for the text creation.

In England and Wales, we are likely to be directed to deliver a lesson on 'spotting fake news' as this forms part of the National Curriculum. There are many fake websites that we can use to show students how easy it is to fall into believing a conspiracy theory or just using information that is wrong. These include: Save the Tree Octopus (https://zapatopi.net/treeoctopus); Dog Island (www.thedogisland.com); and Petrol Direct (www.petroldirect.com). We might decide to engage the class with something in the context of their research; the BBC offers some sophisticated ideas through their specialised website: www.bbc.co.uk/programmes/articles/4fRwvHcfr5hYMMltFqvP6qF/ help-your-students-spot-false-news. If we are willing to take more of a risk and safeguarding concerns have been addressed, we could ask students to create their own fake news sites and try them out on their classmates. ClassTools (www.classtools.net/breakingnews) provides a fake news generator that, like its other products, is similarly not live (so can be used with younger students) but allows participants to interact.

Academic honesty and integrity

Academic honesty and integrity are an important part of any information literacy programme. Although it is not a requirement of the curriculum in England and Wales, learning about citation, referencing and bibliography creation is essential preparation for higher education. It also forms part of the 'taught skills' programme of the EPQ and is a fundamental of the IB Diploma Extended Essay.

Many students have been drilled in not copying and pasting and so they do not realise that it is permissible to quote from sources and include short excerpts in a report. Conversely, they do not understand that even if they paraphrase someone else's work, the source needs to be referenced. Further complications arise with the use of images, especially as younger children are often encouraged to add visuals to work with no acknowledgement. In teaching academic honesty, we need to be aware of two basic aspects:

1 What is permissible.
2 How to construct references and a bibliography.

Plagiarism is defined as:

> The action or practice of plagiarising; the wrongful appropriation or purloining, and publication as one's own, of the ideas, or the expression of the ideas (literary, artistic, musical, mechanical, etc.) of another.
>
> (Oxford English Dictionary, 1989)

It is not the copying that is wrong, but the act of trying to pass off what has been copied as your own idea. There are four main types of plagiarism:

1 Intentional plagiarism. This is the most serious form of academic dishonesty because the culprit is aware of what they are doing but decides to take a risk. In an examination situation, such transgressions are not treated lightly and, if caught, the student may pay a heavy penalty.
2 Non-intentional plagiarism. With this type of plagiarism, the offender is unaware that they might have done anything wrong. This may be because they have not been taught correct procedure.
3 Self-plagiarism. This is when a student writes and submits the same piece of work for two separate formal tests.
4 Collusion. This is the pooling of collective thoughts and writing with others, but then submitting a final report as your own work. This is an increasingly common pitfall as group work gains popularity.

By understanding how to identify plagiarism, we get a better idea of how we can teach staff and students to minimise the risks.

A simple way of introducing students to the consequences of plagiarism is given in the next example:

Ask the class to write their name on the top of a piece of paper. Next, add a title – 'Where I went on my holiday'. Tell them you will time them for five minutes to write as much as they can. (Note form is acceptable, don't worry about spelling.) Next, ask them to swap their paper with the person next to them. Ask them to count the words on the paper and put them in a circle at the bottom. Then, tell them to scribble out the name at the top and write their own name instead. Keep hold of the paper. Compare the papers and each person in the pair whose name is written on the paper with the highest number of words is given lots of praise and congratulations and an award (sweets!).

This exercise was developed by Geoff Dubber from the School Library Association. The exercise can be continued further by exposing the plagiarist. When the students come to the front to receive their award, choose one who you know will be able to enter into the spirit of the exercise and, before giving them the reward, hold them back. Quiz them about the contents of the paper – maybe ask them questions about the flight, people they met, where they ate, etc., and expose their lack of understanding. Then call out the real author to give an explanation and to confront the offender.

An extension of the exercise could be showing students examples of real-life plagiarism. It is a good idea to use scenarios that have meaning in their current lives, so concentrate on popular culture or examples linked with areas of the curriculum they are studying. There are many internet sites listing examples of plagiarists in the news.

Universities also provide support specifically for sixth formers (16–18-year-olds) in understanding how information can be used as part of an academic essay. Newcastle University provide a good example: https://sixthformstudyskills.ncl.ac.uk/referencing/quiz-referencing. For something more light-hearted, the Goblin Plagiarism game can be played individually or as a class (www.lycoming.edu/library/plagiarism-game). Another whole class activity is the 'Jail or Freedom' game (www. authorstream.com/Presentation/SarahPavey-1081155-plagiarism-game-updated).

Considering what is acceptable can also be extended to include copyright. This is an area where we might consider developing a talk for an INSET training day for staff. Many are unaware of what cannot be copied and disseminated without permission. Whilst most government-funded schools around the world are covered by blanket licences, this is not the case in the independent sector. In England and Wales, the Copyright and Schools website gives a good summary (https://copyrightandschools.org).

It is important for us, as librarians, to make best practice explicit through exemplar work, leaflets or displays to supplement the lessons we deliver. We may be able to contribute to or write a school policy on academic honesty to provide guidance for the whole school community. Even if this is not possible, we need to become familiar with what is permissible in the handling of information, particularly as teaching staff may look to consult us as information experts about these matters.

We have already explored how ready-made references can be copied and embedded into a bibliography. Nonetheless, understanding the construction of a reference is an important skill for students to learn, especially if they are headed to higher education. There are many different recognised formats for a reference but unfortunately no real consensus about what should be used when. Swaen (2021) gives a good overview of the rationale behind different options. We can ask departments in the school which style they prefer or consult the exam board syllabus in case there is mention there. Basically, referencing has two major divisions of format:

- Author/Date (e.g., Harvard)
- Footnotes (e.g., MLA).

Generally, we can apply a system whereby for subjects where writing is more minimalised because of the presence of formulae, experimental data and charts, we can suggest an Author/Date system. For more reflective writing analysing texts, we might consider a footnotes system. This is simply because footnotes in a text-based essay help to break up the writing visually. The use of ibid. and op. cit. in footnotes also gives a more academic feel.

Many students and staff assume that the purpose of referencing is simply to show they have not cheated and that they have not made up the information. While this is a valid point, it shows that they do not always understand that a reference enables a reader to find out more about the topic being discussed and also enables an examiner to understand how you have built an argument around a subject and reached a conclusion. A good analogy to use is showing your working out in a mathematics question or providing a sketch book with a finalised art project. By understanding this concept, students can see why it is important for references to contain exact information and be presented in a set order to avoid any possibility of misinterpretation.

Teaching referencing can be a challenge as it is not the most exciting of subjects. Students need to be given plenty of opportunity to practice and therefore ideally it should be a whole school approach. Nonetheless, by using some inventive lesson plans we can make the steps involved more memorable.

The students were divided into groups. Each group was given a source to reference using a given citation style. Each group was also given a set of A4 cards with a different component of the reference on each card, for example, author surname, author initials, date of publication, title, etc. The group needed to work out which cards to use and which to discard and then line them up in reference order. The rest of the class watching could ask to change the order or add or remove items if they felt it necessary. As an added amusement, if the writing was in italics as part of the format, the student holding that card could lean sideways! Students were placed in teams of six. Each team was given a source to reference with a style guide. Each team had some biscuits and an icing pen. They wrote the component of the reference on the biscuit in the correct format and lined up the biscuits to make a reference. The next step, on instruction from the librarian, was for one member of the team to eat one of the biscuits. The group then decided what the impact of the missing information would be on finding the source material. Then another biscuit could be eaten and the discussion repeated.

It is easy to find university sites offering online guidance and games about constructing references to supplement our lessons. However, the key is to practice the skills regularly and to start the process of recording information, at least in a basic format, as early as possible at primary school.

Presentation of information

The overall goal of information literacy and digital literacy is to enable students to become competent and discerning handlers of the ever-increasing amount of information available to them. They will then be able to make informed choices about what to accept and what to use in their own compositions. It is estimated that by 2025 the world's data will have grown to 175 Zettabytes. One Zettabyte is a trillion Gigabytes (Patrizio, 2018) so these skills will be vital.

We can assess how much of what we teach has been understood if we see the end product of their research. Many teachers may just bring students to the library and expect them to cope without instruction and this can be frustrating for us as librarians. However, if we are involved, it is important that we see the process through to the end and ideally are involved in the marking. The end product might be an essay, a slide presentation, an experiment report or even an artefact or a performance.

Learning to put the information that has been found through research together in a coherent order takes skill and this is also an important component of information literacy teaching. By using a mind map creatively, we can show students how to write in a way that will engage their audience.

The students were asked to sketch out a structure for their research write-up using a mind map. They then turned the headings they had written into questions. This helped them understand how a reader can be encouraged to be engaged with the text while seeking an answer to the question, plus how they as the author can work within a boundary without veering into irrelevant information. Later, the headings could revert from the question format.

Structuring an essay in this way at the beginning of the research process also helps students to gather information under the headings either in physical or digital folders. We can show them how this type of organisation can help with the writing and production of the final piece. We might also devise a lesson to explain the differences between types of written report, whether it is a scientific report, a discursive essay, a persuasive text, a narrative account or presenting the pros and cons of a product or situation.

Writing up research is another area where students could be encouraged to use the technology available on their mobile devices. The development of voice to text apps means that students can dictate notes as they read or watch and then the time saved can be used in proofreading and editing. Again, this helps to develop use of their own opinions in their work.

In summary

Information literacy and digital literacy are important life skills. Students need to have a good understanding of what these terms mean and how they will impact on their education, the workplace, health, everyday living and their place in society as a global citizen. To achieve this, we need to ensure they have space to practice these skills and, as librarians, we should show our schools why this is so important, even if it is not taught formally and assessed.

We may not be employed to teach, and we may have little or no teaching experience, but we can learn from our teaching colleagues and liaise with them to deliver these skills. There are many sites available with ready-made lessons that we can use, such as the Times Education Supplement files, Pinterest and Teachers Pay Teachers. Also, organisations such as The School Library Association and the School Librarians Network have data banks we can consult. We might choose to develop our own lessons using one of the information literacy or digital literacy models.

We know we face barriers. The lack of support from formal learning directives means we must create opportunities within the existing framework. This takes time and effort, as well as expertise in communication skills. Secondly, our task can be made more challenging if we are perceived as an adjunct to the English department rather than having a cross-curricular role. However, these are both barriers that can be overcome and by doing so we can develop the scope of our service to everyone's benefit.

Action points

1 Seek out opportunities to deliver information and digital literacy.
2 Liaise with teaching staff who would like to collaborate and aim for a cross-curricular presence.
3 Read the National Curriculum and exam board specifications to identify areas where information and digital literacy skills could be applied.
4 Ask for a slot in a teaching staff training day to emphasise the need to teach and practise these essential life skills.
5 Investigate potential models for information and digital literacy and see what might be used in the context of different subject areas.

6

Using Technology to Enhance the Library Experience

Caroline Roche

Introduction

This chapter deals with the basic technology tools you can use to showcase your library to others. It will also inform you about the role that e-books and online resources can play in your library and what you should look for when choosing the best fit for your school. Remember, it is not only the students who need to know about your library; the parents, teachers and governors can also have a positive influence on your service. Furthermore, using technology can be a great way to connect with authors and publishers.

The library website

Your website is how you show off your library to the outside world, as well as internally to your school. Your library can appear in several different places – on the school website, on the school intranet pages and on your library management system (LMS), if you are hosted online.

One of the first things to establish is whether the school library is mentioned on the school website. If it isn't, then make it your priority to ensure that it can be found there. The library is a major investment for any school and they should be championing the work that you do. Placement is also important – it should be in the curriculum area, not tucked away with sports facilities.

When writing about the school library for the website, make sure you emphasise all the good things you do – author visits, competitions and reading awards, etc. But make it generic – you don't want to have to change the script every year. Ensure that your name is on the entry as well, so parents or other enquirers know who to ask for. And if you have an online LMS then include the link there too. Other information you may find useful to include are opening times, how many items can be borrowed and for how long, and whether the library is open before and after school.

If you have a school intranet then, again, it is important that the library has pages there too. Don't worry if you can't design them yourself, ask for help from the IT department or have a look at other departments' pages and find the one you would most like to imitate. Ask the Head of Department who designed the page if they can give you some help designing yours. The information you have on your page depends on what is usual for your intranet to host, but at the minimum it should: link to your LMS and to any other online subscriptions; highlight information about competitions and upcoming author events; showcase books; and advertise events like Black History Month. Try to make it engaging and appealing, a go-to page for students and staff. It is a great 'shopfront' for all the wonderful things you are doing in your library.

If you have an online LMS and you can design the front page easily, you can also use this to showcase the resources in your library to everyone.

Social media accounts

The first question you need to think about before setting up any account is who are your primary audiences? Who are you intending to reach with each one? For every account, the demographics will be different and you will sometimes need to put different materials up for each one you use.

Twitter

For Twitter, your audience will not be your students. Some sixth formers may use Twitter, but it is not common for any younger students to have a Twitter account. However, you will be reaching the 'outside world' and so this will include parents (including prospective parents), governors, the Headteacher and fellow staff. Twitter is extremely useful for listening to others – especially if you follow fellow librarians and other influencers in education. It is a great place to find out about the latest research and studies and to chat to fellow professionals.

Remember that if you are using your school library account, you must have your professional 'voice' on. This is particularly hard to remember when you are tweeting from home, at the weekends or during the holidays. If you find this discipline too hard to master at first, you could just tweet when in work for several months until you get the feel of your professional 'voice', and then you will be able to extend to weekends and holidays. Bear in mind that what you say reflects on your school and any negative comments may earn a rebuke from the Headteacher. It is also worth remembering that any retweets will be seen as an endorsement of that tweet or blog post – you need to read something carefully before retweeting or commenting. If you are unsure, check out the person's credentials and what sort of things they post about or comment on. If you also have a personal Twitter account, double check which account you are looking at before you say anything!

Use the school Twitter account to showcase any activities and displays you are doing, ensuring you do not show any students' faces so they cannot be identified. It is a great idea to tag any authors or publishers that may be included in the activity or display – they will probably retweet you and comment, which gives your tweet greater reach and publicity. The example in Figure 6.1 below includes people that SLG wanted to retweet the tweet and a popular hashtag so that it would gain visibility. Finally, a picture or a gif always increases the reach of your tweet by making it more visible in people's timelines.

 CILIP SLG @CILIPSLG · 5h   ...
It is a fact, backed up by research, that school librarians will help to support the mental wellbeing of children and young people as they return to schools. Not least by having great books for empathy and diversity. @CILIPinfo @NickPoole1 #covidrecovery

Figure 6.1 *Using images to enhance your Twitter posts*

For more information and advice about Twitter, who to follow and how to use the platform, see SLG's *Key Issues* leaflet on Twitter (https://tinyurl.com/SLGWake).

Instagram

This is the social media account that students are more likely to follow. You will also find publishers and authors on Instagram, so it is a good place to talk about books. Your content will be more visual here than on Twitter. Pictures of displays or new books in the library work well, especially if you tag relevant people for further reach. Be sure to engage with the huge community of book lovers on Instagram by using popular hashtags such as #bookstagram, #yafiction and #mgfiction, etc. You could also set up or take part in an Instagram Challenge where you take pictures on a theme each day. These are great fun and help you widen your circle on the app. All the other guidelines about your professional 'voice' are the same as with Twitter. You can also find an SLG *Key Issues* leaflet about Instagram (https://tinyurl.com/SLGWake).

Facebook

You won't find many young people on here anymore – it is mostly used by older people to share pictures and stay in contact with friends, as well as by small businesses. Of course, you are free to open a school Facebook account, but check first if your school has its own general account and ask if you can put stories on there instead. This will give your stories greater reach as parents probably follow the school Facebook account to find out information about term times, etc. However, Facebook is a good place for you to join support groups and find out information from other professional associations and book clubs, but you must make your own judgments here.

For any social media account you set up, you will first need to check your school's social media guidelines. The school should have a policy on this. You may also need to check with your line manager, or perhaps the Headteacher, before setting an account up so that you have permission to do so (given that you are speaking on behalf of the school). You may have to submit the password to the school, so they can close the account if necessary or pass the account on to your successor. Remember, these aren't your personal accounts, they are run on behalf of the school library.

Very occasionally, you may get abuse on your social media account. Clarity and transparency are by far the best policy. Let your line manager and Headteacher know (whichever is appropriate). Screenshot the abuse, then block the person doing it. Remember, it is (rarely) anything you have done or said, especially if you have been following guidelines. The school will then manage any issues that might ensue.

Online resources

Online resources need not be expensive and there are some very good free resources around. However, if you can persuade your Headteacher or finance manager that buying into one or two paid resources is useful for all subjects, then you are more likely to get funding to cover these resources. You will need to do your homework first and find out what works best for your school. The best way to do this in a secondary school is to talk to the Heads of Department. Find out what they currently use and what they might like to use. If they use online resources for their department already, ask if you can set up a library page that collates all the links to existing online resources. This will keep everything in one place and showcase the usefulness of the library as a central reference point. Also, add links to free resources so that people get used to seeing the library pages as their first port of call. This could be the front page of your LMS, a page on your e-portal or on your website.

How do you decide whether your school needs any online provision? Ideally, all secondary schools with a Sixth Form and Sixth Form Colleges should have online provision as part of training the students for university or any other further education. Online resources play a big part in the university experience and one of the roles of the 21st-century school library is to prepare students to navigate the world of information they will need for work. Just as we teach students the information skills to help them navigate Google, we also need to teach them to search the type of databases they will encounter outside the school environment.

Primary school students will not need to have used the large and expensive databases that secondary students need, but some experience of searching databases, and appropriate word and phrase selection, would be very useful.

All paid databases have a free trial period. Take full advantage of this. Ensure that the teachers who would be using it have the free logins and follow up with a quick questionnaire towards the end of the trial. If there is little enthusiasm for the database, however useful you may think it will be, don't buy the resource. My own experience has shown that if you don't get teacher buy-in to a resource, however good and however much you think it matches their needs perfectly, the resource will not be promoted or used and your money will be wasted. Just put that resource to one side, along with any notes you have made, and try again in a couple of years' time when you may have a different Head of Department or an enthusiastic staff member in that department who will promote the resource.

A good way of managing the cost of databases is to split the subscription with the departments who will be using them. Don't forget, if your school offers Extended Project Qualifications (EPQs) or the International Baccalaureate (IB), many of your paid resources will be invaluable to students.

Although your students will probably go straight to Wikipedia when they have something to look up, you can gently remind them that Wikipedia is crowd sourced and so everything they see there will not necessarily be totally accurate. With older students, it is a good idea to show them 'how to use' tips to narrow down their search terms. Google has a lot of different identifiers you can use to narrow a search down, in addition to the ones underneath the Search bar. Here are a few useful ones:

- Use Google as a dictionary by using Define: word you want to look up, for example, 'Define: alliteration'.
- Use a 'phrase in quote marks' to ensure that the exact phrase is searched for, instead of individual words. Very useful for looking up lines of poetry or song lyrics, for example, 'Lucy in the sky with diamonds'.
- Use a hyphen (-) to exclude certain words from a search, for example, 'dogs–labradors'.
- Use the + sign to be specific about what you want, for example, 'labradors+rescue dogs'.
- To search a particular website, use a colon, for example 'Iraq:bbc.co.uk'.
- Use * to fill in for words that you have forgotten, perhaps in a lyric, such as 'Lucy * with diamonds'.

Although students can use Google to perform mathematical calculations, it is much more useful for them to go to the free website Wolfram Alpha (www.wolframalpha.com) as this is especially built for mathematical and scientific calculations and will have all the information they need.

Another free resource is Google Scholar (https://scholar.google.com), which has a lot of content hosted free, including many academic articles. It has an accompanying site where whole (or more usually partial) chapters of books can be read (www.google.co.uk/books). If students are signed into their own Google account, they can keep articles and books in their libraries to refer back to later. It would be worth your while putting a link to Wolfram Alpha and to Google Scholar on your library pages.

For students interested in art and culture, Google has a free specialist site (https://artsandculture.google.com) that you can direct your students to. This site is more focused than ordinary searching. National Geographic (www.nationalgeographic.com) also has an excellent free site, with beautiful pictures and articles for geographers, artists and scientists.

Politics students may like to know that they can search the House of Commons Library for free (https://commonslibrary.parliament.uk). For Economics students, the Financial Times site (www.ft.com) allows free logins whilst on school premises by using your IP addresses. And for all students, but particularly Sixth Form, schools can also apply to the free Newspapers for Schools charity (https://newslibrary.newspapersforschools.co.uk), which allows access to every single national daily and quite a few regional newspapers as well.

For younger students – Key Stage 3 and below – there is *The Day* newspaper (https://theday.co.uk). DK Find Out! (www.dkfindout.com/uk) is a great site from the publisher Dorling Kindersley and is a simple, visual encyclopedia.

Finally, don't forget to put links to the Khan Academy (www.khanacademy.org), which is great for students eager to learn more about their subjects, and the educational part of TED talks (https://ed.ted.com), as well as the ordinary TED talks for older students. This list is by no means exhaustive and it is worth looking out for other good free sites you can use. Social media can be useful for finding out about these.

As you can see, without having to pay out for expensive online resources, you already have quite a few resources available at your fingertips. If you know there is nothing free to replicate what you want, this will allow you to evaluate carefully which paid online resources you buy into.

E-books

E-books are a good investment for the school, but they are not cheap. There are several providers, all with different business models. Again, it is important to evaluate exactly what you want from an e-book provider and how it will integrate with your LMS. Some of the main e-book providers for schools are Browns Books for Students (www.brownsbfs.co.uk), Sora by OverDrive (www.overdrive.com/apps/sora) and ePlatform from Wheelers (www.eplatform.co). There is one legitimate site with free e-books and that is because the books it contains are now out of copyright. That site is Project Gutenberg (www.gutenberg.org/ebooks).

Copyright, especially of e-books, is something you will need to be acutely aware of. During the COVID-19 pandemic, this issue has been highlighted as access for students to class books has not been possible. Teachers can put pressure on you to find free copies of books on the internet. To make it absolutely clear, there are no legal sites other than Project Gutenberg that provide free books. There are sites on the internet where you can find PDFs of books, but they are all pirated and it isn't legal to use them. You should not co-operate when asked to search for free books and let the teacher know why, or even the finance manager. This is because not only will the school itself be open to prosecution and being fined, but you personally will also be fined heavily for having downloaded the book. You can explain this to the teacher, who can then choose to take the risk themselves. However, it is morally wrong to deprive authors of their livelihoods, so much so that they may not be able to continue writing, and as a librarian you are expected to follow a code of ethics. You can find out more about this code in CILIP's Ethical Framework: https://tinyurl.com/ye2nkjaj.

A similar issue applies to Kindles in the UK. Librarians in other countries will need to check their own Amazon agreements, as publishers have agreed different things in countries outside the UK. At the time of writing, there is no provision in the UK for educational use of the e-books you download onto Kindles. Although you are allowed to run up to six devices using your Kindle account, these must all be registered for your personal use. You cannot therefore buy a book on Kindle and share it with a class load of devices – this is illegal and may open you and your school up to lawsuits and fines. Confusion can arise as you can share books between up to six Kindles registered on the same account, but that is simply for your own or family members' devices. Amazon can, and will, delete all the books you have bought and downloaded if you are in breach of their terms and conditions. The only safe way to have e-books is to buy them through specialist e-book providers. As with online resources, check and see what level of provision would suit your school: some have audiobooks included in the subscription; some need a separate audiobook subscription; some allow online streaming; and with some you must download the book onto your device, thus taking up memory. First, evaluate the needs of your students and how they use their devices – do they have easy access to Wi-Fi at home or do they only use their data on their phones? The best providers allow you to choose either to stream the book on Wi-Fi or download it to your own device.

Many public libraries will provide e-books and other online resources as part of their offering. It is worth encouraging your students to join their local library. They need not borrow physical books from the library, but the online resources, including e-books, can be accessed without visiting the library and are free. The downside of this is that their borrowing will not be counted in your own school library issue figures. However, the advantage is that you will be giving your students access to e-books and other online resources at no cost to you, as well as potentially increasing the range of titles available to them.

Managing technology within your library

Your school will have a policy on the use of mobile phones and personal computers. This is the first thing you should check when formulating use of technology in your library. Some schools have a very strict no phones policy and they will not want you to allow phones under any circumstances. Some schools allow phones at the teacher's discretion in lessons and at the librarian's discretion in the library. If this is the case, some things are still not permitted in the library – for example, gaming, watching videos for entertainment, phoning other people – but others – for example, using Kahoot and other quizzes, looking something up quickly rather than logging on to a computer, taking photos of worksheets to use later, using the phone as a calculator, watching course specific videos with headphones in – are allowed. You must think about what is sensible and will cause you the least work and disruption. The stricter the policy, the harder it is to enforce and the more it will bring you into conflict with students, especially if they perceive you to be stricter than other teachers in the school.

The same thing applies to personal computers. If your school allows students to bring their own devices (BYOD), then you need to consult the school's policy. In general, allowing students to sit on their computers and play games in the library is probably not what you want to happen – and certainly not if you are attempting to establish the library as a place where students read or study. Gaming can become competitive and noisy very quickly. It is much harder to pull back from something you have once allowed than to quietly ease restrictions, so consider the function of your room, make your decisions in consultation with your line manager and stick to the rules, making them clear and enforceable with students. If need be, use the school's behaviour policy to ensure that the rules are taken seriously – although it won't be long before this becomes the 'norm' and students know what to expect in the library.

Other easy to use apps and websites

As you start to become more confident, you will find there are lots of easy-to-use apps and websites to help you reach your students online. Some are instinctive – like Wakelet (https://wakelet.com) – and some will need a bit more practice – like Canva (www.canva.com), which is a good way to produce posters, social media assets, animated resources and comics, although you will naturally get a wider range of uses with a paid account. Any list shared here will soon become out of date, so the best advice is to look out for courses to help you use them and give you ideas, or simply take advantage of free apps and trials to practice things yourself.

Action points

1 Map out what you think should be on your school website about the library. What is already there and how can you improve it? What impression of the library do you want to give?
2 Set up a social media account and plan some tweets or Instagram posts to go on it. Start following some people and just 'lurk' quietly for a while, watching and learning.
3 Investigate your local public library. Will they allow any connections between your students and them? Is the connection easy for the students to use? Would it be possible to have free e-books and online resources via this route?
4 Investigate one of the free websites – Canva or Wakelet – and produce something you can use in your school setting.

7

Equality, Diversity and Inclusion in the School Library

Barbara Band

Introduction

A school library needs to engage with the whole community by providing a supportive and inclusive environment in which diversity is valued and respected; where no student feels excluded, either through a lack of appropriate resources or activities; and where there is an ethos of equal access and participation. This chapter details why a diverse and inclusive library is important by looking at:

- both its intrinsic value and the legal aspects that impact on provision
- what a diverse collection consists of
- other areas of the physical library and library services that need to be considered
- how to analyse the needs of your school community and audit your collection
- sources of resources and information.

The Cambridge online dictionary defines diversity as 'the fact of many different types of things or people being included in something; a range of different things or people' and inclusion as 'the act of including someone or something as part of a group, list, etc.' (2022). From these simple definitions, we can see that a diverse and inclusive library is one that has a wide range of resources and services containing many differing elements that have been selected with consideration to the needs of the whole school community.

Equity is an interesting concept and is different from equality. Equality means giving all students the same support regardless of need, but this does not reduce inequality. The only way to do this is by giving students what they require to bring them up to the same level as others. An example of equity is ensuring disadvantaged students have the same opportunities to access online information as others, regardless of their individual circumstances.

It is impossible to support every student individually with regards to their specific cultural and ethnic needs, individual abilities and interests, so we group our students according to particular characteristics and endeavour to support the priorities of each group. There is nothing wrong with this, but it is important to remember that not all diversity is visible or obvious. Black and Asian minority ethnic students tend to be easily identified, but white ethnic groups such as Irish Travellers are not and so are included within a homogenous mass with other white students, despite having a dissimilar culture and distinct needs. This is also true of disparate religions and many students have a sexual orientation that they prefer to keep private. Thus, it is important to ensure that all aspects of diversity are supported regardless of whether you think they exist within the school community.

Why having a diverse collection is important

There are both tangible and intangible reasons why it is important to have a diverse and inclusive library collection, as well as legal obligations:

1 Diverse books enable all students to explore their identities without comment, criticism or censure. This is an essential aspect of reading for children and young people. Books with characters similar to themselves, or that deal with issues they may be facing, help them to not feel isolated, enable them to investigate their feelings and possibly offer them a solution or resolution. A range of books that feature diverse and inclusive characters, as well as those that explore the traditions and history of other cultures, helps validate students' identities and heritage.

2 It is necessary to have a range of fiction and non-fiction books that allow students to see themselves represented within their community. If students are unable to see themselves characterised, the message they receive is that they are worthless and that their personal culture and heritage is not important or valued. This marginalisation ultimately impacts on their self-worth, affecting their mental health and wellbeing. Students who are different are often, unintentionally, excluded and bullied by their peer groups and a narrow library collection that does not represent the full diversity of the school community will exacerbate this. Such exclusion can lead to feelings of isolation, with further detrimental impacts on mental health and wellbeing.

3 Diverse books bring visibility to different cultures and ethnicities,

helping to build a sense of unity and inclusiveness by enhancing readers' understanding of the experiences of others. Reading about other cultures and becoming familiar with characters that look and behave differently helps to develop empathy and acceptance. If you only read books with characters similar to you or stories that mirror your own experiences, it can lead to a belief that your life situation is more important than others.

4   Students who are socially isolated from the wider world can 'meet' people unlike themselves within books, hence giving a more realistic and truer picture of society. Small rural schools, especially, often have a very narrow demographic. Unless students are planning to live and work within the same community for the rest of their lives, they are going to meet a more diverse range of people than they currently experience. It is therefore important that they understand the world is full of differences from an early age. Books can start discussions about these differences and how they impact on people's lives. Showcasing and celebrating diversity can eliminate barriers, leading to changes in attitudes.

5   Highlighting similarities as well as differences can create understanding. Books that feature multicultural characters as an integral part of the story, rather than the focus of the story being about their issues, enable readers to identify with the fact that all people have dreams, hopes and emotions and that, despite being from a very different cultural background, everyone can feel happy or sad and suffer loss or disappointment.

In addition to these reasons, there are several legal aspects that need to be considered in the context of providing library resources and services.

Human Rights Act 1998

The Human Rights Act became UK law in 1998 and sets out the fundamental rights and freedoms that everyone in the UK is entitled to, regardless of whether they live here, are a visitor or an asylum seeker. The Act contains several 'articles', each dealing with a different right. The Act covers public organisations rather than individuals, but it is worth noting that this includes publicly funded schools. For further information, see the websites of the Equality and Human Rights Commission (www.equalityhumanrights.com/en/human-rights/human-rights-act) and Amnesty International (www.amnesty.org.uk).

United Nation (UN) Convention on the Rights of the Child

This came into force in the UK in 1992 and is the basis for UNICEF's work. The term 'child' covers from birth to 18 years of age. The Convention contains 54 articles covering all aspects of a child's life, but four are seen to be of particular importance:

- Article 2: Non-discrimination
- Article 3: Best interest of the child
- Article 6: Right to survival and development
- Article 12: Right to be heard.

Article 2, non-discrimination, is relevant to school libraries. Discrimination includes: sexism; racism; sectarianism; homophobia; transphobia; and discrimination against the disabled. There are two types of discrimination mentioned. Direct discrimination, where somebody is treated differently because of their race or gender, and indirect discrimination, where rules are in place that apply to everyone but affect some people unfairly. An example of this would be a class set text not available in braille or as an audio book, thus discriminating against students who are visually impaired. For further information, see the UNICEF website (www.unicef.org.uk/what-we-do/un-convention-child-rights).

Equality Act 2010

The Equality Act is an important piece of legislation and lists nine protected characteristics:

- age
- disability
- gender reassignment
- marriage and civil partnership
- pregnancy and maternity
- race
- religion or belief
- sex
- sexual orientation.

The Act means that schools must provide equal access and support to all students; they cannot discriminate against those with a listed characteristic. Schools also cannot provide services or facilities in a way that disadvantages students. For example, books on relationships need to include all types of relationships, not just heterosexual ones.

There are exceptions to the Equality Act. Disabled students can be treated more favourably to put them on an equal footing; for example, you can restrict the loan of audio books to just students with visual disabilities. Faith schools are allowed to discriminate in how they provide education, but they cannot discriminate in relation to the protected characteristics; for example, a Church of England school can visit a cathedral and does not have to arrange visits to other religious buildings. Curriculum content is also excluded from the Act to allow exposure to thoughts and ideas without fear of legal challenges, but the teaching of it needs to ensure that students are not subjected to discrimination; for example, the teaching of relationships needs to be inclusive, include all relationships and cannot imply that some are better than others.

It is also important to recognise that, under the Equality Act, one group cannot deny the needs of another. Thus, for example, a group of parents and carers from a particular religion cannot force the library not to stock books with Lesbian, Gay, Bisexual and Transgender (LGBTQ+) characters using the argument that it is against their beliefs. The Equality Act protects the library from enforced censorship and challenges to resource provision. For further information, see the Equality Act 2010 (www.legislation.gov.uk/ukpga/2010/15/contents).

There are also other legal aspects that cover library provision:

- The Office for Standards in Education (Ofsted) state that the 'school environment should meet the needs of all pupils irrespective of age, disability, gender reassignment, race, religion or belief, sex or sexual orientation' (2022). They will look at behaviour and safety within a school in the context of the Equality Act. Although independent schools have their own inspection body, they use Ofsted measures as a guideline.
- A key component of the statutory guidance for safeguarding is having an equality and diversity policy that seeks to prevent discrimination, harassment and bullying, and details how to deal with these issues. The librarian should be aware of all school policies and how they impact on library provision.

How to ascertain the demography and needs of the school community

Before you can determine whether a library collection meets the diverse needs of a school community, it is necessary to identify and analyse the demographic characteristics of the school population. The needs of the students should inform our decisions, both with regards to the resources we provide, as well as the services we offer. The Equalities Act is a good starting point although some protected characteristics, such as marriage and civil partnership, are not so relevant, whilst others, such as disability and race, need to be expanded to be more useful. Consider the following in relation to the school community:

Age

Although the most immediate thought with respect to age discrimination is against older people, it is important to remember that we have a range of ages within school and that it is necessary to ensure that the ethos of the library does not exclude certain year groups. For example, if the library is always used as a silent Sixth Form study space, including at breaktimes, this could exclude browsing activities by younger students and it may not feel so welcoming to them.

Disability

The definition of disability is a physical or mental impairment that has a substantial and long-term adverse effect on that person's ability to carry out normal day-to-day activities. Disabilities can be visible or invisible. Visible disabilities can be easy to identify, but it is important to remember that others, such as hearing impairment, may not be so obvious. However, it would be usual for the school to inform all staff of any students who need additional support.

The term disability comprises not only physical disabilities but also learning and intellectual disabilities, such as students who are neurodiverse. Neurodiversity covers disorders or conditions where there is a variation in the brain with regards to sociability, learning, attention, mood and other mental functions. This includes Autism Spectrum Disorder (ASD), Attention Deficit Hyperactive Disorder (ADHD), Dyslexia, Dyspraxia, Dysgraphia, Dyscalculia and Tourette Syndrome.

National estimates suggest that over 50% of children who have a disability live on or near the margins of poverty and that 35–40% of children with a learning disability are likely to have a mental health issue. Mencap (2022) states that 351,000 children aged 0–17 years have a learning disability in the UK. The ADHD Foundation is a neurodiverse charity that estimates that one in five people live with a neurodiverse condition, with 2–5% of children and young people experiencing ADHD (2020).

To support these students, it is necessary to know about their conditions and how it impacts on their learning. It is therefore imperative that the librarian is given relevant information and can work closely with the Special Educational Needs Co-ordinator (SENCo) and pastoral team to provide an inclusive library environment for students.

Mental health conditions

Under the Equality Act, mental illness may be considered a disability because its effects can cause impairment to carrying out day-to-day activities. They must be substantial and long-term. The World Health Organisation states that mental health is:

> A state of well-being in which every individual realises his or her own potential, can cope with the normal stresses of life, and can work productively and fruitfully, and is able to make a contribution to his or her community.
>
> (WHO, 2018)

Mental illness is a disorder of the brain function and can range from short-term to severe conditions. Students with mental health disorders are unlikely to reach their full potential, are more likely to suffer from reduced academic achievement and often exhibit poor social and emotional skills. Studies from mental health charities show that mental illness is increasing amongst children and young people, and that children are experiencing poor mental health at younger ages. The NHS reports that 12.8% of 5–18-year-olds have a mental health problem (2017). The mental health charity, Young Minds, suggests that one in eight children have a mental health disorder, with one in six young people aged 16–24 years having symptoms of a common disorder such as depression or anxiety (2022). Minority ethnic and LGBTQ+ students are at greater risk of developing mental health problems due to isolation, discrimination and bullying.

Whilst students with severe mental health problems need specialist help, the school library can support the mental health and wellbeing of all students.

Common mental health conditions include:

- Stress and anxiety: a certain amount of stress is normal and most people have strategies in place to help them cope with it. However, when these are reduced, such as not having enough time to read for pleasure, or when stress factors increase, mental ill health can result, usually in the form of anxiety.

- Anxiety disorders: continual long-term stress can result in anxiety disorders. These can take many forms such as panic attacks, phobias or obsessive compulsive disorder (OCD).
- Depression: is the most common type of mental illness. This is not being a bit low but a persistent feeling of sadness and loss of pleasure in usual activities, with a resulting impact on emotional health.

Race

When people consider race, they often assume it refers to only Black and Asian minority ethnic students, but it is much wider than that. Under the Equality Act, race refers to a 'group of people defined by their race, colour and nationality ethnic or national origins'. Ethnic origins may not be the same as a person's current nationality and can incorporate a person's cultural factors, such as nationality, ancestry and language, plus many people identify with their family's ethnicity. One race will have many ethnicities. It is also important to recognise that a racial group can be made up of two distinct groups, such as British Asians or British Jews. Discrimination can be direct or indirect, such as when policies or rules are put in place that result in a particular racial group being at a disadvantage. Harassment is also considered discrimination.

The 2011 census lists the population of England and Wales as just over 56 million, with 21.3% being under 18 years of age (Office for National Statistics, 2011). There are 23 categories of ethnic groups listed, with 'white' being the largest at 86%. The numbers in other ethnic categories have risen from the 2001 census, with the largest group being Asian ethnic at 7.5% and those identifying as being from a Black African background doubling from 0.9% in 2001 to 1.8% in 2011. This increase is likely to continue and will result in a corresponding increase in ethnic representation within school populations.

In 2017, the Centre for Literacy in Primary Education (CLPE) undertook the first UK study looking at diversity in children's literature. 'Reflecting Realities' quantifies and evaluates the extent and quality of ethnic representation and diversity in children's publishing. The latest report (2020) found that of the 6,478 children's books published in 2019, only 680 featured ethnic minority characters and only 5% had a minority ethnic main character. However, 33.5% of students of school age are of minority ethnic origins. There is obviously an imbalance between the diversity in published books and school populations and the school library collection needs to take positive steps to address this.

Gender and sexual orientation

Sexual orientation is defined as the attraction towards your own sex, the opposite sex or both sexes. The government estimates that 5–7% of the population are LGBTQ+ and Stonewall, an LGBTQ+ charity, supports this figure. Numbers are difficult to ascertain, especially amongst children and young people, because:

- people keep personal information private – this is due to many reasons, for example, they may fear bullying or they may have family who would not support them
- they have not yet decided who they are
- the terminology used in data collection can skew results – if the only gender choice is male or female, there are no means to collect an accurate representation of the LGBTQ+ community.

The school library should support all students regardless of their gender, including those undergoing gender reassignment. Additionally, it is important to ensure that the ethos of the library, including the signs and language used, does not reinforce gender stereotypes.

Creating a diverse collection

Having undertaken an audit of the school population to establish their needs, the next step is to carry out an audit of the existing library resources to identify gaps. You can only ensure you have a collection that meets the needs of the community if you know what is missing and you will only know what is missing by ascertaining what you already have. Once you have looked over the collection with a critical eye, it is easy to identify gaps, for example:

- Do your geography books cover all the countries and heritages of the students? Do you also have books featuring celebrations, festivals, art, food, myths and legends from those countries? Even if your school population has a narrow demographic, it is important to have a collection featuring a wide range of cultures.
- Do you have up-to-date history books so that students can explore their family's heritage? It is important that history books present an accurate view of events and are not written from just a white perspective.
- Do your books (fiction and non-fiction) depict different identities and experiences, such as a range of skin colours, hairstyles, family structures, home lives, spoken languages, abilities, customs and beliefs?

- Do you have a range of books on different religions or just focus on those covered within the curriculum? It is not always possible to tell what religions students follow so it is important to have resources on all of them.
- Do your illustrated science books show both girls and boys carrying out experiments? Are the scientists featured diverse?
- Are your careers books inclusive or do they imply certain careers are only suitable for girls or boys?
- Does your biography section contain a wide range of diverse and inclusive people? Real life stories can be powerful, enabling students to recognise others in similar situations to themselves and helping them realise there are solutions to the issues and problems they face.
- Do you have any titles that specify gender, such as *Drawing for Girls* or *Cooking for Boys*? Books that promote stereotypical roles should not be on the library shelves.
- Do your health and sex education resources include all types of relationships or do they just cover heterosexual ones?

A useful way of checking your existing stock is to undertake a diversity audit whereby you take an analytical look at the collection to determine its representation and identify any areas lacking in diversity that need developing. Furthermore, it can be worthwhile to measure the collection against booklists such as those featured on Love Reading 4 Kids (www.lovereading4kids. co.uk) (see below for further booklist suggestions). These will help you identify any books you already have that encompass diversity and inclusion and provide ideas for future purchases. As well as considering the depiction of diversity within books, it is necessary to have a wide range of minority ethnic, disabled and LGBTQ+ authors and illustrators. If you have a local Schools Library Service (SLS), they can provide advice and recommendations to ensure your collection is diverse and inclusive.

Just because a book is popular, has been used as a class text for years or is on a recommended reading list does not necessarily mean it should continue to be used or kept in the library. Many older books used within schools or included on reading lists depict discrimination and bias – these should be assessed according to the Equality Act and its protected characteristics and removed or replaced if necessary.

Ensuring the library collection is diverse and inclusive is a continual process. It involves not only checking existing stock, but also measuring any new purchases against required criteria, keeping in mind all aspects of possible discrimination. Terminology changes. Words and phrases become unacceptable. It is imperative that you keep up to date with current thinking and continually monitor your stock against the acceptable norms of society.

Things to consider when purchasing new stock include:

- How are the characters portrayed? Are both males and females given stereotypical roles? Are females always given a secondary role? For example, are girls depicted as being helpless and not very clever, waiting for 'the boy' to come and rescue them? Are boys always the character who solves the problem?
- Does the story exhibit bias or discrimination? Are minority ethic characters always in trouble at school or carrying out crimes? Are the minority ethnic or LGBTQ+ characters always killed off first? Do the LGBTQ+ characters always have family problems with coming out? Whilst students sometimes want to read about others experiencing similar problems, this is not always the case. Too often, stories revolve around differences and the issues people face. Inclusivity means that characters fit into the story and are not simply an add-on to include an element of diversity.
- Do picture books and illustrated stories show a range of family situations and diverse characters? For example, do they always show mum doing the cooking and dad washing the car? Or mum staying at home and dad going out to work?
- Book covers are important. Whilst it is true that sparkly pink covers will often attract female readers and can be used to good effect for this reason, it is important to ensure that not all the stock can be divided into male/female lists by their covers. Characters on book covers should also depict a range of diversity and not a 'perfect' media image or family.

Having a diverse and inclusive book stock is only part of creating a library that is welcoming to the whole school community. There are other aspects that need to be considered such as: terminology; the physical space; displays and promotion; activities; and library policies. Your aim is to remove barriers to make the library a welcoming and accessible place for all.

Terminology

The terminology you use is important. Words matter and it is easy to send subtle messages without realising it. Do not divide boys and girls up when in the library or when collecting information. For example, instead of creating a 'Top ten books read by Year 7 boys' list and a 'Top ten books read by Year 7 girls list', have a 'Top ten books read by Year 7' as this does not label the books in a gendered way. Think about the keywords you use when labelling shelves, creating posters and cataloguing books. Ensure that these reflect all aspects of diversity and use the correct terminology.

Physical space

The physical layout of the library should be conducive for use by all students. Is it accessible for everyone, including those with physical disabilities? You may not have any current students with limited mobility, but in designing and creating a library, long-term use should always be considered. If the library is not placed on the ground floor and has no lift access, students who cannot use the stairs will be unable to reach it, including those temporarily using crutches. Are the shelves the right height so all students can reach all the stock? If the shelving is too high and the library cannot be rearranged or new shelves purchased, it may be that the top shelves are only used for display purposes.

Think about book labels, shelf labels and signage: are these in dyslexia friendly fonts and colours and are they large enough for students with visual disabilities to read? Are the classification systems in use easy for students to understand? If you have decided to use the Dewey Decimal Classification (DDC) for non-fiction stock, there is a simplified version for use in schools, particularly at primary level.

The physical library space is also important for the mental health and wellbeing of many students. For those suffering from poor mental health, the library can be a refuge, a quiet and safe area to escape to with a supportive member of staff who will listen. The library can also provide resources in the form of books, information about self-care and helplines to outside organisations. Try to incorporate different areas within the library to accommodate a range of activities, including quiet reading, individual study, group work and collaborative activities.

Displays and promotion

Books need to be actively promoted so that students are aware of them, otherwise resources will remain hidden and unused. Displaying and promoting diverse books has a big impact on the school population and helps to ensure that different cultures and ethnicities are seen as part of the school community. Consider all aspects of diversity when promoting library resources. Think about the diversity of authors and illustrators when creating a display or booklist to promote a specific event, such as Science Week, and ensure you feature minority ethnic, disabled, LGBTQ+ and female scientists – your display should not just consist of old, dead white men. Promote your diverse stock amongst staff so they can, in turn, promote it to the students.

Monitoring the use of the library and resources can help to highlight underused areas of stock, as well as groups of students who do not use the library. If these are from a specific group, for example, an ethnic group, boys from a particular year group or SEN students, you can use this data to help create promotions targeted at these groups to raise awareness of what the library can offer them. It may be that this underuse has highlighted a stock gap which your local SLS or school book supplier can help you with.

Activities

Although it is natural to organise library activities and events based around books and reading, consider extending these to appeal to a wider range of students. This may require collaboration with other staff and departments, but it can help to reinforce the message that the library is a whole school resource and not simply an extension of the English department. Creating an annual calendar of events can help to give you an overview – ensure that it is diverse and inclusive, incorporating different religions and cultures.

Don't have every competition based on creative writing. This often excludes those with SEN so consider something that requires a piece of artwork to be submitted or non-fiction writing, such as producing a news report, so other styles of writing are validated. If you run events that include food, make sure you incorporate different dietary requirements; these could be religious, as well as lifestyle choices. Don't put everything online as this excludes those without internet access at home.

Organise wellbeing activities, such as reading for pleasure book groups, craft sessions and other creative events to support students.

Library policies

It is important to have policies that detail how the library deals with stock selection, donations, weeding and complaints, especially with regards to diversity and inclusion. Having policies in place and ensuring they are supported by senior management will allow the librarian to meet any challenges or complaints about specific material. Although it is tempting to accept any donations, especially when budgets are restricted, all books should be checked against the same criteria and donors need to understand that unwanted or unsuitable books may be sold to raise funds for more up-to-date texts or given to charity.

Staying up to date

It is important to keep up to date with events and discussions that may impact on the diversity of your collection. Involve the student voice in book selection. Be aware that terminology changes or may vary in different countries. For example, in the UK the term 'BAME' has often been used but generally replaced with 'ethnic minority', whereas in the US other races are referred to as 'People of Colour' (POC). Develop your knowledge of the different aspects and challenges around diversity by signing up for newsletters from relevant organisations, reading reports, articles and blogs on their websites, and following them on social media.

Action points

1 Undertake a diversity audit of your student population in terms of ethnicity, cultures, religions, SEND and neurodiversity.
2 Check your non-fiction resources to ensure you have these aspects covered, for example, books on different countries, books on world festivals, books about neurodiverse conditions, etc. Use the suggestions above for further ideas.
3 Check the gender representation within your non-fiction stock and remove any that only have stereotypical images.
4 Use the links in the Further Reading section below to access lists for suggested diverse books and check your stock against these.
5 Think about your library displays for the coming year and plan to ensure that a diverse range of titles, authors and images are included.

Further reading

A Mighty Girl – www.amightygirl.com
   A collection of empowering resources (including books) that offer positive messages about girls and their diverse capabilities.
BookTrust – www.booktrust.org.uk
   BookTrust is the UK's largest children's reading charity. Their resources include several booklists on different themes and a book finder that enables you to search the booklists using specific keywords and age ranges. BookTrust also publishes 'BookTrust Represents' (www.booktrust.org.uk/what-we-do/programmes-and-campaigns/booktrust-represents), a regular report on the representation of people of colour among children's book creators in the UK, and 'Breaking New Ground' (www.booktrust.org.uk/globalassets/resources/represents/breaking-ground-brochure.pdf), a brochure that highlights over 100 minority ethnic writers and illustrators.
Books For Keeps – http://booksforkeeps.co.uk
   An online magazine with reviews for books, from under 5s to young adults, as well as articles on related topics. The website is searchable by keyword.

Books for Topics – www.booksfortopics.com

Curated and up-to-date booklists on a range of topics, suitable for primary school children.

Inclusive Minds – www.inclusiveminds.com

A collective for people who are passionate about inclusion, diversity, equality and accessibility.

Love Reading 4 Kids – www.lovereading4kids.co.uk

A large recommendation site with book reviews, ranging from toddlers to teens, from librarians and schools. There are fiction and non-fiction booklists, which can be searched by age and keyword.

Love Reading 4 Schools – www.lovereading4schools.co.uk

Companion site to Love Reading 4 Kids, this website contains booklists according to school years and topics.

Reading Zone – www.readingzone.com

The aim of this website is to help young people, parents, adults and teachers find out about children's books.

Toppsta – https://toppsta.com

Book reviews organised by age range, reading lists for year groups and selection lists based on specific topics.

8

Advocacy, Marketing and Evaluating your Library
Lucy Chambers

Introduction

This chapter looks at how school librarians can plan, market, evaluate and demonstrate their value and impact. It also considers how you can advocate for your role and why this is important.

Advocacy

Research shows that school librarians can make a difference to students' educational standards:

> Strong school libraries are linked to important indicators of student success, including graduation rates and mastery of academic standards. The most substantial and consistent finding is a positive relationship between full-time, qualified school librarians and scores on standards-based language arts, reading, and writing tests, regardless of student demographics and school characteristics.
>
> (Lance and Kachel, 2018, 1–2)

However, there is little UK evidence-based research about the impact of school librarians, a situation that threatens jobs and contributes to negative public opinions about their necessity in the internet age.

> The visibility of librarians in society presents a paradox . . . [There is] potential for the profession to drift and its value and recognition in the world to slowly dissipate.
>
> (Lawton, 2016, Preface)

What is needed across the entire UK is a school library strategy as demonstrated by Scotland in its *Vibrant Libraries, Thriving Schools* report (Scottish Library and Information Council, 2018). It is not enough to know that the school librarian's work makes a difference and to assume that school stakeholders appreciate it. This knowledge must be demonstrated and communicated within and beyond the school, in fact to governmental level – a mission undertaken by the Great School Libraries campaign (www.greatschoollibraries.org.uk):

> All children deserve a great school library because adequately funded, staffed school libraries deliver enhanced and independent learning as well as reading and curriculum support. School libraries contribute to building lifelong readers and support whole school initiatives promoting reading for pleasure. All of this evidence shows us that school libraries are a vital part of every school, and should be cherished and maintained.
>
> (Great School Libraries, 2019)

School staff may have little idea of what a librarian can achieve, their cross-curricula role and their specialist skills of improving the uptake of wider reading and teaching vital information and research skills.

Case study 8.1: Comments from two school librarians about the early days of their first posts, expressing the difficulty of being new solo librarians

It was a difficult start. I wish I'd seen that I would be on my own. There was no previous librarian to support me. I was fumbling around in the dark. A year on, I've been told by students and staff that I've done a good job.

I fell into the librarian role during a restructure. I had no prior experience of how the various aspects of the job fitted together. There was a legacy of the role being handed out to anyone who showed an interest with no direction and no training. I had to be driven and proactive. I wish I'd known that the role was pretty much there for me to shape as I wished.

Both librarians became proactive and more confident as they gained experience in their roles and undertook external training. It is up to every school librarian to demonstrate their impact both within and beyond their school for personal advocacy, for promotion of the library and its services and for wider activism.

Case study 8.2: Advocacy from a primary school Headteacher

The work of a school librarian has the potential to make a huge contribution to the school in ways that I had not realised until we found ours. Her work has impacted directly on the children, their involvement and enthusiasm for reading, as well as our participation in enrichment activities and the maintenance of the reading environment.

Case study 8.3: Advice from a school librarian on the importance of communication with staff

List everything you do each term and flood the Senior Leadership Team (SLT) and Heads of Year with it. It can lead to more use of the library – more bookings, because it only takes one member of staff to see how well a particular event went and they then might just want a piece of it too. Your hard work is worth shouting about – otherwise nobody would know . . . what you did, and they need to.'

Here are some examples of advocacy:

- Websites for campaigns, such as Great School Libraries, and librarians' blogs:
  — Find quotations about reading and educational outcomes to use in reports to SLT; base library objectives and initiatives on published research.
- Posters linked with research, such as the School Library Advocacy Deck produced by CILIP School Libraries Group (SLG) and the National Literacy Trust (Humphrey, 2021):
  — Display advocacy posters in the library and around the school.
  — Use research quotations in reports to justify your objectives and initiatives.
- The CILIP SLG 'To Do Well at School' leaflet (SLG, n.d.) explains why every school should employ a librarian and how librarians help schools achieve educational outcomes, promote wellbeing, develop reading for pleasure and information, teach information skills and provide safe spaces:
  — Give to parents at school events.
- Librarian-led staff training:
  — Promote library facilities to staff.
- School library branding (see below):
  — Use to visually promote library facilities on communications within and beyond the school.

- School social media accounts, school website and school blog:
  - Promote library facilities.
  - Use the library brand.
- School librarian's blog:
  - Promote library facilities to whole school community.
  - Issue reading lists for curriculum topics, book award shortlists and reading for pleasure genres.
  - Cite recent literacy research relevant to the school and library.
- Positive reports in articles and on social media promoting the school's achievements:
  - Promote the school and library to the wider community.
- Stories and comments from students, staff and librarians:
  - Use positive comments in reports to SLT as qualitative data for evaluation and to promote library facilities.
- Signage in libraries and around the school incorporating pro-reading phrases:
  - Promote the importance of reading and advocate for library facilities.
- Marketing campaigns (see below):
  - Communicate with library users and non-users to learn more about their learning and reading needs.
  - Improve library facilities.

Here are some examples of advocacy that school librarians can create to demonstrate the effectiveness of their role:

- writing case studies for the Great School Libraries website
- writing articles for the librarianship and educational press
- writing impact evaluation and reports of library activities for the school SLT and governors
- talks at education and librarianship conferences/other CPD
- blogs and social media.

Marketing

Marketing is part of a strategic planning process and contributes to deciding how to achieve library objectives. It is far more than just the promotion of individual activities. Promotion is part of a marketing framework and one step in the marketing cycle shown in Figure 8.1 opposite. Use marketing techniques to discover who your library users are, their needs and how you can provide targeted library services.

Marketing is taking steps to move goods from producers to consumers. It's determining what people want, delivering it, evaluating consumer satisfaction and then periodically updating the whole process (Dempsey, 2009, 13–24).

Figure 8.1 *The Cycle of True Marketing*

Figure 8.1 demonstrates the process of marketing your library, evaluating success and planning improvement (Dempsey, 2009). The Cycle of True Marketing was created by Kathy Dempsey, founder of the Libraries Are Essential consultancy, for her book, *The Accidental Library Marketer* (available online at www.librariesareessential.com/library-marketing-resources/cycle-of-true-marketing).

Start by working out the current facilities of your library. You could go through a self-evaluation process (see below) or use a strengths, weaknesses, opportunities and threats (SWOT) analysis:

- Strengths: What do you do well currently?
- Weaknesses: What do you not do so well? What further training, practice or resources do you need?

- Opportunities: What objectives would you like to achieve?
- Threats: What barriers are there to achieving your objectives?

Your marketing plan is related to your general library objectives. These are based on the school's targets, mission or School Development Plan and your vision for the library.

Think about what you are trying to achieve. You might be:

- trying to bring in new students or staff:
  — who visits the library and why?
  — who does not visit the library and why not?
- encouraging current students to take part in more activities or a specific activity:
  — which specific user groups should you target?
  — why are you targeting them?
- encouraging students to read specific book collections or use online resources:
  — who needs these resources and what benefit will they gain from using them?

Ensure that objectives are quantifiable and time limited. For example, one objective might be: 'I would like to increase readers of my new Empathy book collection by 20% by the end of term'.

Knowledge about library users and their needs gives you the background you require to target activities related to your objectives. You can also target specific groups, which is a process called segmentation. Use surveys, focus groups and conversations to find out which specific library services are used by different user groups and what they need. After analysis of the responses, you will have some quantitative data (numbers of responses to particular questions) and qualitative information (comments). The easiest way to survey users and analyse data is using an online survey tool, such as SurveyMonkey (https://www.surveymonkey.co.uk).

Teachers are usually busy and a library survey is unlikely to be a high priority for them, so it may be better to talk to people directly. By being visible in the staff room you get to know the teachers who never visit the library and can steer the conversation round to what you are trying to find out. This informal approach enables you to ask staff about what they are working on, which can provide ideas for new library services and activities. As a school librarian says: 'Find out what teachers need so you can offer support then you'll have a much better chance of showing people how necessary you are.'

Here are some tips for written surveys:

- Think about what you are trying to find out and frame the questions accordingly.
- Avoid ambiguous questions.
- Keep the survey short.
- Allow the option for respondents to add comments.
- Comply with GDPR rules.

Use a focus group to gather subjective (qualitative) data from individuals; include a range of departments and students from all year groups. Consider carefully what you want to find out.

Case study 8.4: Use of a focus group

I helped advise a school about re-establishing its neglected library. We set up small focus groups from three different year groups to discuss views on the current library, what experience of school libraries students already had, book genres they enjoyed and what features they would like in their new library. The answers varied for each year group and provided valuable qualitative information for the final report to the Head.

While you are discovering information for a specific purpose through focus groups, surveys and talking to people, you are also promoting your library, your skills and advocating for the profession. The next stage is to decide on your actions and to write a marketing plan setting out who you are targeting, why, with what activities, the timing and how you are going to evaluate your success. Gather feedback when you have completed your project and use this to evaluate its success and to inform future planning.

Once you have decided on your activities, you need to advertise and promote them. Proactive school librarians already promote their initiatives but may not do so in a strategic manner.

Promotional tools include:

- posters and leaflets explaining library procedures
- signage – promote particular collections using a catchy name
- library branding (see below)
- newsletters – place a link on the school website's library page
- displays in the library, around the school and in the staffroom
- student voice – a student library committee and reading champions
- sessions showcasing the library for staff
- family reading groups, family events and parental borrowing

■ screens around the school
■ competitions – display the entries around the school and on social media
■ speaking at school assemblies, parents' evenings and other school events
■ social media (see below)
■ writing copy for local newspapers about library events and speaking on local radio.

Online promotional tools are even more useful as you can gather analytics data to assess interest in your promotion and attract a much wider audience, providing greater advocacy for your school. Examples include:

■ a library page on the school's website and Google Classroom
■ digital content:
— animated videos and e-content
— library podcasts
— videos of information and research skills lessons
— Wakelets, Padlets and Sway presentations.
■ visual lists of resources in the library
■ links on your website page
■ social media, a library blog, Twitter, Instagram – all valuable tools to share information about your library and resources with the wider community.

Creating a library brand and identity is a very effective way of promoting your library visually to the whole school community. You may need to include your school's logo or its colour scheme in your library logo. Add a suitable positive and snappy slogan to promote what school libraries offer and what your vision is.
A library logo and/or slogan:

■ makes your library instantly recognisable
■ can help build goodwill and familiarity
■ is a simple way of keeping a high profile
■ demonstrates your expertise
■ demonstrates your range of activities
■ advocates for school libraries
■ promotes reading.

Case study 8.5: Two school librarians talk about library branding

'Our logo is on all our notices and signs, certificates and publications, and on slides displayed on plasma screens around school. It was designed by our Graphic Design and Communications Manager when we wanted to re-launch the library with new behaviour expectations. We also have a READ logo which was the winner of a student competition. We use this on any posters, publicity or slides to promote reading. Both logos are also included on slides used in our library lessons and presentations, so students are very familiar with the library brand.'

'I branded our library after two sites merged. I ran a competition for all students to design a logo, judged by the art teacher. We tweaked the winner's logo slightly and came up with a picture of letters falling out of a book with our school name on top. The colours were part of the uniform that students wear. I use this logo in all our communications – in school letterheads, a logo rubber stamp that is stamped on the stamping sheets inside covers of our stock, promoting competitions, school end of term newsletters, on the SharePoint page, etc. This identity now sets us apart from other departments and is immediately recognised as the library.'

The key is to incorporate promotional tools into a marketing strategy so that your objectives can be achieved, evaluated and adapted for the future.

Evaluation

Librarians regularly write reports to showcase their activities and the current state of the library. School libraries should ideally be included in the school's own evaluation processes so that the library is part of the school review and development planning system. However, specialist library evaluation is necessary too, as the library is not tied to one department but is a central service and very different to other academic areas of the school.

Self-evaluation is a method of demonstrating the success of various criteria such as space, teaching and library resources. It is a model used by the SLS-UK Library Awards scheme, where schools achieve different levels of awards for their libraries, depending on their facilities and activities. The aim is 'to recognise the work of the library in school to support pupils and help raise achievement' (ASCEL, n.d.). It encourages schools to develop their libraries to a high standard, using detailed criteria, including library stock levels, staffing, opening hours, the space, working with staff and whether the library has a library management system (LMS).

Impact evaluation goes further because it attempts to measure how your work has made a difference to the library user, rather than being a benchmarking exercise. Impact evaluation includes using quantitative (statistics) and qualitative (comments) evidence. It is a tool encompassed in the Theory of Change (ToC). ToC is a structured framework planning process to measure change, available online at www.theoryofchange.org.

The industrial language of impact evaluation (input/output/outcome) can be off-putting. The most important concept is that instead of evaluating what you do day-to-day (processes/output), you need to look at what you achieve (outcomes) and for whom (stakeholders). By considering this from the planning stage you can then decide what data (evidence) you need to collect to demonstrate what difference your work makes (impact and value).

You can find templates and worked examples in the NHS Toolkit (https://kfh.libraryservices.nhs.uk/value-and-impact-toolkit), which, although not about school libraries, provides clear explanations of evaluation processes. The Toolkit 'provides an outcomes-based, rather than process-based, approach to evaluation' (NHS Knowledge and Library Services, 2021). Streatfield and Markless' book *Doing Library Impact Evaluation* (2022) includes examples from school libraries and other sectors.

Undertaking impact evaluation demands thought and planning. Using a visual planning template is essential. Concentrate on one or two objectives rather than attempting to analyse your complete library service, particularly if you are a solo school librarian.

At the planning stage decide what you are trying to achieve, your marketing and promotion strategy and how you will collect and analyse evidence of success. Gather evidence from when you start implementing your activities. Undertake before and after surveys of your students to measure change, for example, in attitudes to reading.

From the outset consider:

- what you want to achieve (vision) rather than what you are going to do (process)
- how to measure impact (indicators)
- what difference this activity will make and to whom (stakeholders)
- which objective this activity relates to
- what evidence you should collect and how
- what outcomes you are expecting
- what criteria will determine success.

Collecting evidence is the same for both self-evaluation and impact evaluation. The difference lies in how you make use of the data and what conclusions you can draw.

When planning your library year of teaching and events, consider what outcome you hope to achieve by offering initiatives, then find activities that will generate evidence to demonstrate this. For example:

- shadowing a book award impacts on literacy and oral/communication skills
- holding an author visit increases enthusiasm for books leading to wider reading and improved educational outcomes
- running fake news and other information skills lessons contribute to improved research skills, leading to independent learning skills.

The more usual way to look at this is starting with the objectives and offering suitable measurable activities. For example:

- objective 1: improve learning outcomes
  - activities: develop suitable curriculum resources by discussion with Teacher Leads; teach information skills lessons with all year groups
- impact evaluation measurement: skills analysis spreadsheet; questionnaire
- objective 2: improve student book choices for reading for pleasure and information
  - activities: provide resources that are current, appropriate to age and ability, fit for purpose, inclusive and diverse, accessible, relevant to curriculum and interests
- impact evaluation measurement: track selected students' book choices over several terms; reading attitude survey.

Some practical ideas include:

- Activities based on a timetable of national events related to reading, such as Empathy Day, World Book Day (WBD) and the Yoto Carnegie and Kate Greenaway Medals.
- The local public library or Schools Library Service (SLS) may mount regular activities that you can join in with; their evaluation questionnaires provide data for your evaluation report.
- Base the timing of activities on specific events in your school's calendar, such as open days, book week (this is often planned around WBD) and other celebrations or charity events.

A planning sheet incorporating evidence gathering, marketing and success measures is essential. The key is to use terminology and techniques that help you with the process.

Case study 8.6: A planning tool

I devised a planning spreadsheet, based on the School Development Plan but incorporating library-specific impact evaluation and marketing, to plan activities linked to objectives and to create data for impact evaluation reports. The headings include:

- group/class
- objectives, timescale, costs
- initiative/information skills lesson/project/club name
- marketing and promotion plans
- expected/actual outcomes/success measure (before and after)
- impact statistics used/measured impact/response numbers
- student/staff/stakeholder comments
- evaluation/reflection
- future actions.

Structured planning makes my part-time role manageable and enables me to work effectively towards my vision for the library's central role in the school.

Quantitative and qualitative responses are equally valid. It is important to use the same parameters each time you run your data analysis so that you can compare it over time to measure change. The Reading Outcomes Framework Toolkit links objectives to relevant published research and is a good source of questions (Reading Agency, 2016).

Collect statistical data, such as the number of book loans by different year groups, from your LMS. Some LMSs are automatically updated with student data from the school administration system. This may include whether a student is EAL, Pupil Premium or SEN. This is useful for analysis purposes (ensure you conform to school data privacy policies). If the LMS statistics reports do not go to this level of detail, with some specialist knowledge you can extract the information onto a spreadsheet and conduct your own analysis.

Whenever you help a user, ask them how they made use of the information and what they thought about the service. Feedback is valuable qualitative research. You could design a simple feedback form. Write evidence from day-to-day conversations or observations in a notebook. Comments contribute to stories showing impact on individuals. Here are some examples of evidence:

- questionnaires:
  - reading attitude surveys
  - tests of prior knowledge and what was learnt from library lessons
  - focus group questionnaires designed to elicit opinions
- interviews and conversations with individual students:
  - collecting stories
- observation of students – how they interact with the initiative:
  - write a case study about working with an individual student
- talking to teachers about students
- measuring/judging reading levels and interest levels
- look at students' work throughout the initiative:
  - include class marks or comments written on work
  - include feedback from teachers, students and parents
- library data from the LMS and digital platforms
- social media analytics data
- loans statistics:
  - class/group rankings
  - data about targeted groups.

Case study 8.7: Using evidence to inform future planning

Free Writing Fridays: The librarian ran this project because the school had a focus on raising achievement and developing independent learners, also on literacy and developing creative thinkers. It was based on resources by Cressida Cowell for non-assessed creative writing and drawing. 35 to 40 students attended weekly sessions, with all materials supplied free. A short questionnaire each term was handed out to ascertain student enjoyment and helped guide developments for future sessions. It generated very positive responses from students and staff.

Student comments included: 'a great opportunity to explore your imagination'; 'it's so nice to relax, draw and write with nobody telling you what to do'; 'I love getting good ideas and being able to share them'; and 'I hope to achieve becoming a more developed writer.'

Staff comments: 'This allows students of all abilities to feel included and involved in a safe space; the LRC space allows them to have access to resources and minds they may not ordinarily access.'

(Taken from the Great School Libraries case studies, available online at
www.greatschoollibraries.org.uk/case-studies.)

Impact evaluation reports enable librarians to communicate the value of their work to the school. Summarise your key findings and what you intend to do next (Markless and Streatfield, 2013, 164–179):

- Keep reports short.
- Break up text with bullet points.
- Include relevant official research quotations.
- Infographics are very effective, colourful and compact.
- Include both quantitative analysis and qualitative data.

Evaluation, like marketing, is a continuous process. Compile evidence throughout, reflect on what went well, what was not so successful and re-evaluate as necessary, as shown in Figure 8.2 below.

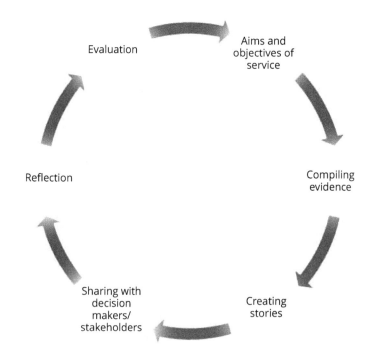

Figure 8.2 *The evaluation cycle* (Source: CILIP Impact Toolkit Evaluation Cycle (CILIP, n.d.))

Create case studies from your data using the Great School Libraries website template. Place stories highlighting how you helped students on school websites and on social media. They are brilliant advocacy and promotion not only for your efforts but also for the school itself.

Case study 8.8: Stories demonstrating impact

From a fathers' event at a primary school:

> The father figures commented that they would never have spent so much time in school if it wasn't for these events; dads clearly feel part of the school community now. One quote from a child regarding the breakfast together event: 'I was hoping he would come. I don't get that much time to have a one-to-one with my dad, so it was good to spend time with him.'

From a fake news library lesson at a secondary school:

> Student's comment: 'I have learned that you should always do your research and check other reliable sites to see if they have also written about the article. If they haven't, and nobody else has, it normally means it was made up.' Feedback from teachers has been very positive, they have all reinforced how much students need this type of lesson in order to be well informed and responsible digital citizens.
> (Taken from the Great School Libraries case studies available online at www.greatschoollibraries.org.uk/case-studies.)

Visual presentations of statements and data break up text and have a more immediate impact than description. Turn data into graphs and pie charts using tools on a word or data processing package. There are many examples online. Logic models show impact over a longer timeframe and are useful for broad, generalised concepts. An example is in The Reading Agency Reading Outcomes Framework Toolkit (Reading Agency, 2016, 4). This shows on one page how reading activities lead to greater reading engagement outcomes. Infographics show statistical and descriptive information in a succinct and visually strong manner. An example from the *American Libraries* magazine uses simple statements, silhouette illustrations and statistics to show that 'School librarians improve student achievement' (SinhaRoy, 2016).

Conclusion: the strategic school librarian

To be effective, school librarians need a structured long-term approach, with vision, planning, measurable objectives, marketing, promotion, reflection and evaluation. Look beyond day-to-day management of the library space and take a detached stance. The key is to incorporate the most important elements of marketing and impact evaluation cycles into a practical template and to translate the jargon into workable tools. What makes a difference is putting library work into context in a strategic management framework, measuring impact and sharing the results with key stakeholders, the wider profession and beyond for advocacy purposes.

Action points

1 Create a planning spreadsheet for one of your current objectives, incorporating marketing, promotion and evaluation.
2 Prepare a pitch for the SLT or a school assembly on a new initiative. Include its objective and how it will impact students.
3 Demonstrate how shadowing a book award has impacted students. What sort of evidence do you need and how will you collect it? Sketch out some ideas for gathering quantitative and qualitative evidence.
4 Create a school library logo and branding statement.
5 Write a case study about a recent initiative using the template on the Great School Libraries campaign's website. See www.greatschoollibraries.org.uk/case-studies.

Acknowledgments

The author would like to thank all the primary and secondary school librarians quoted from the School Librarians' Network and the Great School Libraries website. The author has included some of their own examples too. Special thanks to Kathy Dempsey for adapting 'The Cycle of True Marketing' for this chapter.

Further reading
Advocacy

Great School Libraries (2019) www.greatschoollibraries.org.uk/case-studies.
IFLA School Library Advocacy Kit (2018) www.ifla.org/publications/school-library-advocacy-kit.
Lawton, A. (2016) *The Invisible Librarian: A Librarian's Guide to Increasing Visibility and Impact*, Chandos.
Markless, S. (ed.) (2016) *The Innovative School Librarian*, 2nd edn, Facet Publishing.
Teravainen, A. and Clark, C. (2017) *School Libraries: A Literature Review of Current Provision and Evidence of Impact*, National Literacy Trust.

Young, T. and Lance, K. C. (2016) *School Libraries Work! A Compendium of Research on the Effectiveness of School Libraries*, Scholastic Library Publishing.

Evaluation

ASCEL, SLA and CILIP (2021) *Primary School Library Guidelines – Judging Success*, https://primaryschoollibraryguidelines.org.uk/policy-and-planning/judging-success.

Scott, E. (2009) *Quality and Impact: Evaluating the Performance of Your School Library*, School Library Association.

Shaper, S. (ed.) (2014) *CILIP Guidelines for Secondary School Libraries*, Facet Publishing.

Marketing

Doucett, E. (2008) *Creating Your Library Brand: Communicating Your Relevance and Value to Your Patrons*, American Library Association.

Potter, N. (2012) *The Library Marketing Toolkit*, Facet Publishing.

9

The Primary School Library

Lucy Chambers

Note on the terminology used in this chapter: The term 'primary school' encompasses any primary and preparatory (prep) school setting. The term 'primary school librarian' encompasses any adult who runs a state or independent primary school library, from a trained and/or qualified librarian to someone with no prior experience of the role.

Introduction

This chapter explores primary school librarianship issues, including essential skills; library resources; support organisations; developing the reading culture; information skills teaching; and the differences between primary and secondary school libraries and non-library-based book collections. Case studies based on primary and prep school librarians' experiences are included to provide context.

It is hard to generalise about primary school libraries as each one is run in a different way with variations in their size, stock and staffing. This whole book is relevant to primary school librarians. The aim of this chapter is to look at some key issues rather than to offer a comprehensive guide to how to set up a library. For information about establishing and running a primary school library, see the ASCEL, SLA and CILIP *Primary School Library Guidelines* website (https://primaryschoollibraryguidelines.org.uk), the LIPSSEE website (https://preplibs.wordpress.com) and the references listed in the Further Reading section at the end of this chapter.

Some UK primary schools do not have a library. Others may not employ a dedicated school librarian. Few have a full-time, trained librarian. The library may be the responsibility of the literacy co-ordinator with a teaching assistant

(TA) looking after it for a few hours a week in between their other duties. The Great School Libraries survey findings show that just 38% of primary schools with library space have a designated librarian, as opposed to 95% of secondary schools (Great School Libraries, 2019). This disparity may have a negative effect on students' enthusiasm for reading at primary school, particularly for those from disadvantaged homes and those who do not own books. One in eight children who receive free school meals do not own a book, with one in eleven of all children claiming not to have any books at home (National Literacy Trust, 2018). There is currently 'significant inequality of provision in different Nations and between independent and non-independent sectors [which] points to a clear picture of inequality of opportunity – in turn, impacting on social mobility in disadvantaged communities' (Great School Libraries, 2019). As author and Children's Laureate (2019–22) Cressida Cowell says,

'Children's reading for joy is one of the two key factors in children's future economic success. There is vast inequality in the current primary school library provision' (Cowell, 2021).

School librarians in primary and secondary schools usually have the same vision:

> Adequately funded and staffed school libraries deliver enhanced and
> independent learning as well as reading and curriculum support; they contribute
> to building lifelong readers and support whole school initiatives promoting
> reading for pleasure.
>
> (Great School Libraries, n.d.)

Differences between primary and secondary school libraries

While they have similar aims and vision, primary school libraries differ from secondary school libraries. Primary schools deliver teaching through curriculum-based topic work, rather than using textbooks, and the library stock needs to support the topics taught. Primary school libraries are generally smaller with more soft seating and fewer desks; these library spaces may not be large enough to accommodate a whole class. They may have no computers for student use and may not be the silent study space they sometimes are in a secondary school. The library space may have a carpeted area for groups of children to share books or be read aloud to, much like in a primary school classroom. Shelving bays in a primary school library need to be lower than those in a secondary school library.

Case study 9.1: Moving from a secondary school library to a prep school library

The secondary school library was a silent working space. In the prep school, I maintain a 'library voices' culture. We have regular timetabled lessons for guided reading and library lessons for all year groups.

(Prep school librarian)

Through-schools (schools for students aged 3–18) have both a primary and a secondary school. Both may have libraries, but often the primary school does not have a qualified or trained librarian, whereas the secondary school usually does. In some through-schools with more than one library, there is good communication between the librarians so they can offer joint events, for example, author visits. In others, all the libraries are run by the same librarian. Some through-schools use the same LMS in all their libraries, some just have one in the secondary school library. Some academy trusts share their librarian between schools. Other trusts have individual librarians – often with very diverse budgets and support within their schools. A joint vision for enhancing the school's reading provision and communication between the different librarians can bring whole school benefits, such as easing the process of transition from the primary school to the secondary school and providing a more cohesive selection of texts for whole-class reading.

Research shows that school libraries make a difference to students academically.

[They] . . . impact pupils' general academic attainment, reading and writing skills, plus wider learning skills. School libraries have also been found to have an impact on pupils' reading enjoyment, reading behaviour and attitudes towards reading. Self-esteem and the feeling of success and accomplishment have also been associated with school library use.

(Teravainen and Clark, 2017)

The sooner students are given access to a wide range of carefully chosen and diverse books, the more opportunities they have to become fluent and wide-ranging readers: 'Children need to be enthused to read and if they are, this will become a springboard for their achievements throughout the curriculum' (All-Party Parliamentary Group, 2011). Scotland's national strategy for primary and secondary school libraries, 'Vibrant Libraries, Thriving Schools' (Scottish Library and Information Council, 2018) is a valuable tool for integrating primary and secondary school literacy aims.

Essential skills for primary school librarians

Running a primary school library is a role with many responsibilities. Primary school librarians often work alone and may have no contact with other librarians. Networking opportunities and support from trained librarians may be available in areas with Schools Library Services (SLS), School Library Association (SLA) local branches and via online forums.

Primary school librarians, like secondary school librarians, need specialist librarianship skills for which training is recommended. Specialist skills include organising, cataloguing and classifying; providing and promoting diverse, inclusive and multicultural books; and running the library management system (LMS).

School librarians should be creative and communicate well with students, staff and families. They should read, discuss children's books and have ideas for developing the school's reading culture, while also understanding literacy, the school's curriculum and education issues. School librarians need to be able to evaluate their work in written reports for the Senior Leadership Team (SLT). For a primary school librarian's job description and person specification, see the SLA website (www.sla.org.uk/support-for-primary-schools).

Primary and secondary schools can undertake a self-assessment exercise examining the quality of their libraries via the SLS-UK Library Award at three levels: Developing, Establishing and Enhancing. For more information, see www.ascel.org.uk/sls-uk-school-library-award. This is a useful exercise, giving guidance on how the library could be improved.

Reading for pleasure peaks at ages 9 and 10, with girls aged 7 to 10 reading the most (Eyre, 2021). The quality and diversity of book stock and other resources in a primary school library, and the expertise of the librarian running it, are therefore incredibly important:

> The choice of books and how they are presented is central to success and needs to be tailor-made for each individual school community – and this means the most crucial element of the school library is the librarian running it – the person who brokers that interaction between the children and the books.
>
> (Harris, 2021)

The ongoing sustainability of a primary school library depends on the expertise and vision of the school librarian and how much time they spend running the library; on support and collaboration with school staff; and on the range and quality of books and other resources. The library caters for readers at all levels, including reluctant readers; students with learning difficulties; EAL students; emerging readers; and confident readers.

It is better to have fewer exciting-looking and well-displayed books than many out-of-date and tatty books. Picture books should face forward in kinderboxes. Early readers and short chapter books, young fiction, older fiction and picture books for older readers should be arranged alphabetically by author. Information books covering curriculum subjects and general interest topics are classified with simplified Dewey numbers and coloured labels to show broad subjects. Often there will be subject index sheets on display to guide students. Other essential genres include poetry; myths, legends and fairy tales; graphic novels; cartoon books; dual language books; dictionaries; atlases; and children's magazines and newspapers. Primary school libraries may also contain audiobooks, DVDs, access to e-books and details of websites with online content related to children's resources. A visit to the showroom of a library supplier or large bookshop shows the range of books available for primary schools.

The library should look attractive, well-stocked and maintained and be logically arranged to encourage students to find books that interest them. The librarian might arrange some popular books by genre, for example, fairy tales, comic books and adventure books, to encourage less confident readers to select a book. Books should be catalogued on the LMS.

Primary schools usually follow a curriculum for key subjects based on the National Curriculum. An example from a primary school states that their curriculum:

> . . . is based on the National Curriculum and includes RE, and Philosophy for Children. We are a silver Rights Respecting school and our curriculum reflects the culture, values and the ethos of our school. Our curriculum is designed to prepare our pupils for the opportunities, responsibilities and challenges of life in modern Britain.
>
> (Globe Primary School, www.globeschool.org.uk/Learning/Our-Curriculum)

The English curriculum covers literacy, writing and reading skills. Schools decide exactly how they are going to teach this, many using various commercial schemes for different ages and reading levels, as well as encouraging reading for pleasure with class libraries and a whole school library. For a detailed explanation of how one primary school teaches English throughout the school, see www.globeschool.org.uk/Learning/Phonics-and-Reading. This also covers how reading is promoted throughout the school, including several mentions of its library.

The librarian should have an annual budget sufficient to provide resources and books to support the curriculum and wider reading for the whole school. Often the primary school library budget is small, so librarians need to be inventive. Ideas include running book fairs where commission is paid in free books, asking for support from the school's governors or Parent Teacher Association (PTA), applying for grants and encouraging the school to join the local SLS to borrow resources. It is important that librarians can select books that will be enjoyed by students and that reflect the values of the school.

Support and training for primary school librarians

Several organisations support school librarians (and other teaching staff) by providing practical information about how to set up and run a school library, specialist training courses in librarianship skills and resources for library clubs. Some organisations specialise in primary schools, others support both primary and secondary schools. Many offer a school or a personal subscription and some provide free resources. Schools subscribing to a SLS can receive support – from advice about choosing books to designing the library – and staff can borrow fiction and information books related to curriculum topics and for general reading. The SLS may also offer activities to develop reading for pleasure and resources, such as current reading lists by age and topic. Some SLSs offer consultancy and the services of a trained librarian to strategically manage the primary school library on a long-term basis. See Tower Hamlets SLS for an example: www.towerhamlets-sls.org.uk/plips. Appendix 7 lists organisations supporting primary schools and primary school librarians.

Other literacy organisations support both primary and secondary schools. For example, the Empathy Lab (www.empathylab.uk) produces annual reading lists of books supporting empathy and Letterbox Library (www.letterboxlibrary.com) offers multicultural books for different age groups. Appendix 8 lists literacy organisations for primary and secondary schools.

It is important for school librarians to keep up to date with children's books. Appendix 9 lists selected sources of information about children's books.

New school librarians can learn about essential librarianship skills by undertaking an online modular training course. Below are some courses specifically aimed at primary school librarians:

- The SLA's Learning about Libraries (Primary) course covers many aspects of primary school librarianship in online modules – www.sla.org.uk/course/learning-about-libraries-primary-core-modules
- The National Literacy Trust's Love our Libraries online training is for primary school staff to develop reading for pleasure and some librarianship skills – https://literacytrust.org.uk/programmes/love-our-libraries

- Opening the Book – www.openingthebooktraining.com/en-uk/courses/primary-school-library-training.

CILIP's SLG, YLG and the SLA offer short courses and networking opportunities for all school librarians.

The role of the primary school library and librarian in education

The school library is part of the picture of a school's effectiveness in literacy in the widest sense, encompassing reading for pleasure, interests, information, the curriculum and lifelong learning:

> A school library's role is to inspire and excite young readers and meet their educational demands.
>
> (*Primary School Library Guidelines*, 2022)

Some primary school librarians run guided reading sessions for students and follow prescriptive school instructions, including how to question children to improve their decoding and comprehension skills. In other schools, TAs and teachers conduct guided reading sessions, with librarians not involved at all in teaching literacy skills in this way. Primary schools teach early literacy skills through phonics using government-approved schemes. They may also use other ability-levelled schemes to develop reading and writing skills. Many schools house reading scheme books in classrooms or elsewhere in the school and encourage students to borrow free-choice books from the library.

The primary school librarian has a pivotal role in offering a long-term vision of wider literacies, moving on from mastering the basic skills. They aim to develop enthusiasm for reading by offering freedom of choice of reading material. School librarians provide a safe library space for reading to:

- develop reading for pleasure, interest and information
- encourage the development of creativity, imagination and writing skills
- develop information literacy and research skills.

These key development areas prepare students for the transition to secondary school and lifelong learning. A good primary school library provides a perfect opportunity for students to choose a wide range of books at an age when many students are still keen on reading and exploring information, not just for the curriculum but for its own sake. Students need good reading skills for every curriculum subject:

Frequent reading should be a priority. It should happen not simply in English lessons but also in other subjects such as History, so that pupils learn from what they read.

(DfE, 2021c)

School libraries and librarians can change students' lives:

Libraries allow children to ask questions about the world and find the answers. And the wonderful thing is that once a child learns to use a library, the doors to learning are always open.

(Bush, 2002)

Developing the reading culture in a primary school

Collaboration and support from the literacy co-ordinator and other staff to keep reading at the top of the agenda are important. The primary school librarian can work with different age groups in different ways to encourage whole school reading. For example:

- set up a book swap or lend books to families from a trolley in the playground; run drop-in sessions for families in the library
- visit Early Years to read stories aloud to the children: rhyming stories, story props and stories with actions work well
- organise a creative writing or book-based art competition with younger students
- shadow a book award and run reading and research clubs with older students.

The Reading Framework: Teaching and Foundations of Literacy (DfE, 2021d) discusses how to teach early reading. It acknowledges the importance of reading for pleasure; high-quality talk in a language-rich environment; high-quality adult/child talk interaction; staff reading books aloud to students; the importance of re-reading stories; and the importance of students listening to stories and introducing them to more advanced vocabulary and ideas than they can read for themselves. Many of the concepts can also be applied to older primary school students.

Developing reading for pleasure and encouraging all students to read broadly are of key importance in primary schools:

Reading for pleasure is associated with higher levels of literacy achievement. Those who are good at reading do more of it: they learn more and expand their vocabulary and knowledge. This enables them to understand more of what they read.

(Hayes, 2021, summarising DfE, 2021d)

A proactive school librarian can influence the school's approach to its reading culture:

The work of a school librarian has the potential to make a huge contribution to the school in ways that I had not realised until we found ours. Her work has impacted directly on the children; their involvement and enthusiasm for reading as well as our participation in enrichment activities and the maintenance of the reading environment.

(A primary school Headteacher cited on Tower Hamlets SLS website,
www.towerhamlets-sls.org.uk)

Case study 9.2: Developing reading for the whole school – by a primary school librarian

To create a buzz about reading, I ran a series of reading events. Some examples – Mothers' Day: mothers and children read books together, drew portraits of each other and played word games. National Poetry Day: a children's poet ran workshops on humorous poetry, the school's first author visit for several years. Summer Reading Challenge: I invited a children's librarian from the local library to talk at assembly and at a parents' evening. Many families signed up. Book clubs: Years 5 and 6 took part in the local SLS book award. They performed a short play I wrote about one of the books. I ran a Chatterbooks club and received sets of free books for children to review. I kept some for the library and gave the children the rest. I turned the breakfast club into a breakfast book club by applying for a grant. Children helped stamp and label the books, which got some socially deprived children who owned no books keen on reading for the first time. National Non-Fiction November: Years 3 and 4 shadowed the SLA Information Book Award. They previously thought information books were boring but after this found they loved them. Staff as reading role models: I put a set of shortlisted children's books in the staffroom to get staff reading and discussing them with their classes. Children read more when they discovered that their teachers also loved books. The key for the librarian is to foster good communications with staff and promote books and the benefits of reading to the whole school community at every opportunity.

Many children's book awards include a category suitable for primary school students and have useful resources on their websites. See Appendix 2 for national book initiatives and Appendix 3 for examples of national book awards. For more ideas, see Chapter 4: Creating a Reading Rich Environment.

Information and research skills teaching

Primary school libraries may be seen as supporting reading rather than teaching and learning. However, primary school librarians often teach information skills, from formal whole class lessons to helping individual students. Some information skills are covered by the curriculum and taught in class. Most primary school librarians teach basic book skills, such as how to handle a book, tidy the library and use the LMS to issue books. Tower Hamlets SLS provides an information skills curriculum that builds on core library skills. It aims to:

> . . . improve pupil research skills, enable pupils to evaluate information they find on the internet and in books, improve pupils' overall reading skills, enable pupils to better select their own reading books, encourage the use of the school library within the teaching of the wider curriculum, and to provide skills for pupils to take forward to secondary education.
>
> (Tower Hamlets SLS, 2021)

Case study 9.3: A school's view of a prep school librarian

The librarian is seen as an expert by school and parents in all things books and reading. I work in close collaboration with staff right across the curriculum including subjects like Science and Drama and Learning Support. My role is very hands-on. I have great staff support for events arranged by the library such as book fairs, author visits, World Book Day and family events. Reading is seen as vitally important; children must have a book on them at all times. We get to know our pupils and their reading habits well and offer pastoral support too.

(Prep school librarian)

Case study 9.4: A day in the life of a part-time primary school librarian

I work here one day a week, so I train staff and students to use the library independently. First thing, I meet teachers to discuss shadowing a book award and curriculum books to borrow from the SLS for the classroom collection. Nursery, Reception and two special needs classes visit. I showcase fiction and information books and read stories aloud. Children browse and borrow. Later my team of pupil library assistants help with book processing, displays and shelving. They love being the first children to handle new books and are great at promoting books to their classmates. Then a drop-in session for reluctant readers doing a reading drive. After lunch, 30 minutes free to write a library blog for families. Year 4 visits in two groups, followed by after-school Research Club. We research and write encyclopedia entries about favourite animals and they set each other quiz questions. I spend an hour tidying up, planning a family reading event later in the term and ordering the book award shortlist to be loaned to the class whose teacher I met earlier. This school has a strong reading culture and I love working with children who are so enthusiastic and eager for knowledge and with the very co-operative staff team.

(Primary school librarian)

Classroom and other book collections

The Reading Framework: Teaching and Foundations of Literacy (DfE, 2021d) talks about the importance of the quality of books in primary school classroom corners and class libraries. Some teachers are very knowledgeable about books and have excellent classroom collections with a wide range of stock. Other classroom collections may be less well looked after. Classroom collections are organised by type of book or broad genres, so that all information books can be shelved together, but not in Dewey order as they would be in a school library.

The school librarian (with sufficient time) can look after class collections by removing old and tatty books and topping up from the library. A primary school library is more comprehensive and organised, so that users can find a range of books and other resources on a specific subject or by a particular author. Ideally, a primary school should have both classroom collections and a school library to ensure children have a wide choice of reading material.

Teacher resources are usually kept in a dedicated room and organised by the literacy co-ordinator, subject teachers or sometimes by the librarian. Primary schools may also have levelled readers, which are arranged by colours and numbers for different reading abilities; readers for phonics teaching; big books, which the teacher shares with the whole class (many schools use online resources instead); guided readers – in sets for use by small groups of students; resources for curriculum topics – mixed resources including books, artefacts and posters; class sets – up to 30 books for a whole class to read; and a teacher education collection. There might also be books to be read aloud to classes; other special topic-based collections; posters about different topics; and school archive material.

Pupil library assistants (PLAs)

Many schools invite a team of students to help in the library. Primary school students enjoy the role as it gives them a sense of empowerment and involvement with books.

Case study 9.5: PLAs as Reading Champions in a primary school

My team of PLAs all love the role. They come weekly to shelve, tidy and process new books. I noticed that their classes started to borrow more books, so I made all the PLAs Reading Champions too. They now promote books to the whole school in assemblies, create displays in the library and around the school and write short book reviews, which are displayed on the bookshelves. PLAs have many ideas for promoting books and reading and have enhanced the library in so many ways. I run a training scheme for them to show them other library processes and they love suggesting new books to buy.

(Primary school librarian)

Conclusion

Words are POWER. The more words you give kids, the more interesting and intelligent the thoughts they can have. Books are transformative magic because of their unique ability to develop three magical powers: intelligence, creativity and empathy.

(Cressida Cowell – Children's Laureate 2019–22 (CLA, 2019))

Primary school librarians help develop the school's reading culture. They can teach information skills; empower PLAs; prepare students for transition to secondary school; and work with teachers and families to improve literacy in the widest sense. Their vision for developing reading in the library is based on school objectives, but they also look at the bigger picture, beyond mastering literacy and on to preparing students for lifelong learning and wide reading – both vital for students' access to the curriculum and their future success.

Action points

1 What different resources do you have in your library? (For example, short chapter books, graphic novels, etc.) How do you organise, shelve and label them?
2 Create a poster promoting your library to families. What are its key selling points?
3 Design a lesson plan for students of any age about how to find non-fiction books using a subject index or the LMS. Why is it important for students to learn to search the catalogue?
4 Design an application form for selecting a team of PLAs. What jobs would you like them to do? What personal qualities should they be able to demonstrate?
5 Visit the Primary School Guidelines (https://primaryschoollibraryguidelines.org.uk) or LIPSSEE website (https://preplibs.wordpress.com). Read about a subject you are unfamiliar with. How will you use this knowledge in your library?

Acknowledgements

Many thanks to Denise Reed of LIPSSEE and to all the librarians on the School Librarians' Network forum and from other contacts who responded to requests for their experiences in primary and prep school libraries. This was invaluable for research and some of them have been quoted anonymously.

Further reading
Setting up a primary school library

Braidley, L. S. (2021) *Transforming Your Primary School Library*, National Literacy Trust blog, 21 June, https://literacytrust.org.uk/blog/how-to-transform-your-primary-school-library.

Tarrant, A. (2021) *Ten Tips for Creating an Unforgettable School Library*, BookTrust blog, 26 April, www.booktrust.org.uk/news-and-features/features/2021/april/ten-tips-for-creating-an-unforgettable-school-library.

Thompson, A. (2019) *Creating a Primary School Library*, Library Lady blog, 27 January, https://alibrarylady.blog/2019/01/27/creating-a-primary-school-library.

Running a library

CILIP School Libraries Group Key Issues leaflets, https://slgconnect.org.uk/979-2.

Reading for pleasure

CILIP School Libraries Group Book Chat Packs. Discussion packs based on themed fiction for book groups for primary and secondary schools, www.cilip.org.uk/members/group_content_view.asp?group=201313&id=742276.

Clark, C. and Teravainen-Goff, A. (2018) *School Libraries: Why Children and Young People Use Them or Not, Their Literacy Engagement and Mental Wellbeing,* National Literacy Trust, https://files.eric.ed.gov/fulltext/ED593893.pdf.

National Literacy Trust (2019) *Gift of Reading: Children's Book Ownership,* National Literacy Trust, https://literacytrust.org.uk/research-services/research-reports/gift-reading-childrens-book-ownership-2019.

Williams, A. (2021) *Get Everyone Reading – A Primer on Reading for Pleasure,* www.sla.org.uk/get-everyone-reading.

10

Moving On: CPD and Qualifications

Caroline Roche

Introduction

You have survived your first couple of years in the job and now you want to go further and learn more. This chapter focuses on where you go from here. You may want to look at ways to get more qualifications and training – this chapter will help you think about your career progression. This section is specifically UK-based, however many non-UK libraries are affiliated to CILIP and school librarians have completed Chartership in different parts of the world. If you are not based in the UK, please contact your local Library Association to discover routes that suit you.

As mentioned elsewhere in this book, you will find a lot of quick information at your fingertips in the SLG Key Issues series. There is a Key Issues leaflet on 'Getting Qualified' written by Sarah Pavey, one of the authors of this book. You can look at and download the Key Issues leaflets here: https://slgconnect.org.uk/979-2.

Getting qualified

As the 'Getting Qualified' leaflet points out, there are many different qualification routes you can follow. You can get an academic qualification, which would be an undergraduate degree or a postgraduate degree via full-time or distance learning. This gives you sound theoretical knowledge and will allow you to explore librarianship in depth. CILIP have a list of providers of these courses on their website (www.cilip.org.uk/page/ProfessionalRegistrationLevels).

However, be aware that none of these courses are specifically school library-related, although there will be plenty of information you can relate back to your role as a school librarian. A lot of library work is the same in any venue, for example, the concept of organising resources through a catalogue and classification mode. You will also be more able to move between different sectors of library work, including health, law, pharmaceuticals or academic or public libraries, with one of these qualifications.

Another route to follow is a more practical, vocational based qualification. If you look at the 'Getting Qualified' leaflet, you will see there are courses available – although some have yet to be accredited by CILIP. However, that needn't stop you if you wish to take one of those qualifications. The Open College qualification comes highly recommended by participants. Apprenticeship at Level 3 is a general library qualification, equivalent to A Levels, but it is heavily biased towards information literacy and the practicalities of librarianship, rather than fiction selection and understanding, and so may be of limited use to school librarians (although some academy chains have adopted it). Be aware too that with an apprenticeship you are learning on the job and, strictly speaking, need to be reporting to or working with an experienced librarian and have the opportunities in your job description to fulfil the criteria needed for the qualification.

As members of CILIP, the authors of this book would highly recommend that you apply for either CILIP Certification or Chartership – whichever you feel is appropriate. These qualifications are practical and work-based, but they also show how you are applying CILIP's Professional Standards and Ethics to your everyday work. The Professional Registration Levels page on the website explains more about the difference between Certification and Chartership (www.cilip.org.uk/page/ProfessionalRegistrationlevels).

You can easily start with Certification and move on to Chartership. These qualifications will show your commitment to the profession. Although not all jobs require Chartership, the better paid jobs – usually in private schools or abroad – will generally specify Chartership in their person specifications. As you can see, it is well worth joining CILIP and becoming Certificated and then Chartered as your next step.

The process of chartering generally takes about 18 months, depending on you. CILIP has advisors to help you through this and you can also choose to have a mentor to motivate you if you wish. If you do choose a mentor, it is best to choose someone from a different sector than your own, as this can bring a lot of insight into how other library services operate. You may also be able to persuade your school to pay for your Chartership application, although the cost isn't very high compared to the cost of other qualifications.

Case study 10.1: From NVQ to Chartership

Marina (not her real name) was a full-time mum with four children. She decided to get a job as a library assistant and completed her NVQ2 and 3. She then went on to Certification and Chartership. Now she is Head Librarian of a prestigious independent school, a post she probably wouldn't have been able to achieve had she not been Chartered.

You may be reading this and weighing up whether it would be easier and cheaper just to do a few courses to extend your knowledge in certain areas. These, of course, would be useful, but what they won't give you is a solid basis in librarianship – the sort of knowledge that will allow you to make a real difference in your school and to the students you serve. However, they can be used as evidence as part of the Certification or Chartership process, so are worth doing alongside a qualification. A professional qualification will enable you to speak authoritatively about literacy and learning, holding your own amongst your teacher colleagues. Teachers respect qualifications – it is what they spend their lives doing, after all – and you will find that respect for you and your opinions will grow as you show them you are qualified to bring your thoughts into the conversation.

Working towards Chartership will also give you the opportunity to talk to and work with librarians from other parts of our profession, as one of the parts of completing your Chartership asks you to look at the wider picture. This wider connection to your profession can be very useful and could allow you to move around jobs in librarianship – maybe into public libraries, college or university libraries, or other specialist libraries. Joining CILIP will give you that breadth of opportunity, even if, at the moment, you feel you want to be the best school librarian you can be and that's enough!

Case study 10.2: Courses aimed at teachers

John has been a librarian for three years and is starting on his Chartership journey. His Head of English wants him to be more involved in literacy planning and so John seeks out a course that will help him. He can only find a course aimed at teachers, but his line manager reassures him that this is the best course. Once John has completed the course, he is able to tie in events in the library to the whole school literacy plan, and, as a result, he is also able to suggest ways other departments can use the library to increase literacy in their subjects as well.

Conference events

A big event in the school librarianship world is conferences. The CILIP School Libraries Group (SLG) Conference is held around Easter time every other year. Other conferences are held at different times of the year. The other conferences you could consider are LILAC (Information Literacy Group Conference); the Federation of Children's Book Groups (FCBG) Conference; the Youth Libraries Group (YLG) Conference; and the School Library Association (SLA) Conference. All of these have different themes and styles and you should look at all the programmes carefully before considering which ones to attend.

The advantage of attending the YLG, FCBG or LILAC Conferences is that you will meet librarians outside of the school 'bubble' and so will be able to grow your network successfully. Conferences are excellent places to network and make new friends. At one of our SLG Conferences you will always hear from new and established authors and get a chance to have a signed book from the bookshop. You will hear the latest thinking and research from the world of education, plus there will be inspiring workshops.

However, the costs of conferences are high as they usually involve staying away a night or two. Your school may baulk at the cost – although the cost of a librarians' conference is nothing compared to what a school would pay for a teacher's CPD. SLG knows how hard it is to persuade your line manager that a conference provides good value for money and so we have produced the following impact statement, which you are free to use and adapt.

Attending the SLG Conference: impact statement

Many schools are cutting their training budgets for all staff, so how do school librarians persuade their SLT that the SLG Conference is an essential CPD opportunity? What will schools gain from sending their librarian? The SLG Conference is the key academic opportunity for professional librarians who contribute to the teaching and learning of their schools, as well as providing an essential library service for staff and students. You will take back invaluable knowledge and ideas to implement in your school. You will also evaluate and develop what you already do, leading to both professional development and improvement in your library's contribution to the school.

When booking the conference, your seminars should be carefully chosen with your Library Development Plan and the School Development Plan in mind. As we tell our students, if you know what you want to find out, you are more likely to be successful. A host of leading academics, educationalists and authors make every conference an unmissable event. It provides excellent networking opportunities with librarians from across the country, many of whom are leaders in their field. Those librarians undergoing Certification or Chartership will benefit from an excellent CPD event, as well as being able to discuss library and education issues with their peers.

Continuing Professional Development (CPD): short courses

Short courses are excellent for gaining specific information about what you need to learn. Post-pandemic, there are more online courses than there ever were and they are usually cheaper and much more convenient to attend than in-person events. Often, you will find that if you pay for and register on a course, you will be allowed digital access to it afterwards so that you can catch up in your own time if you don't manage to attend. It is always worth checking this out beforehand though, as it isn't the case for all providers.

You will find that whatever library management system (LMS) you use, there will be further training courses offered by them. Other providers, such as CILIP, SLG and SLA, provide short courses that are worth investigating too. There are also local SLSs who run courses. In addition, unions, such as the National Education Union (NEU), have good CPD for librarians. If you work in an IB (International Baccalaureate) School, there are courses specifically for school librarians for PYP (Primary Years Programme), MYP (Middle Years Programme) and Diploma level – these are listed under teacher training on the IB website (https://ibo.org/professional-development).

Another provider of short online courses is the Open University. You may have already completed our Badged Open Course on the OU platform, FutureLearn (www.futurelearn.com). The courses are free, but you can also pay to upgrade to get certification and other benefits – that is your choice. There is a wide range of free courses on FutureLearn that impact our job – just type 'reading' into the search bar to see what comes up. These can be documented and used for your Chartership application or for your own school's internal Annual Review. Ensuring that you are constantly learning is a great way to show your school that you are professional and a committed learner.

CPD: professional reading

Professional reading is often the headline that people worry about when undertaking their Chartership. They imagine that they will be expected to read a lot of academic reports with lots of unfamiliar terms in, but that isn't only what professional reading consists of. Professional reading is reading about your profession – articles about school libraries, schools, education and libraries and applying that reading to your own school situation. CILIP's *Information Professional* magazine has lots of great articles that can spark an idea for your own school situation, as do the blogs, articles and Twitter feeds of others as well. All reading like this counts so long as you reflect on what you read and have a chance to apply it to your own situation.

Case study 10.3: Professional reading in action

Susan reads an article in *Information Professional* about the opening of a new children's library in a public library. It grabbed her interest because she has the chance to use some money to upgrade her own school library. In the article, Susan reads something about how they made their signage inclusive to all comers. Susan looks at her own signage and realises that it looks tired and probably isn't inclusive. There's a link in the article to a page on the internet where inclusive signage is explained further, so Susan reads up about it there. As a result, Susan puts in a bid to the school to replace her own signage and can justify this with the information she got from the website. Susan is then able to write this up as part of her Chartership submission, explaining how her professional reading brought about change in her own school library.

Once you are Chartered, and therefore are asked to revalidate every year, you will be able to add any professional reading you have done to the list of things counted for revalidation. Not all professional reading leads to a change in your own library, but it all leads to background knowledge you can draw on when you need it later in your career.

There are some websites worth bookmarking that regularly provide great information for school librarians. Keep an eye on these:

1 SLG Connect – https://slgconnect.org.uk – the blog of CILIP SLG. Lots of great ideas here!
2 National Literacy Trust – https://literacytrust.org.uk. It is well worth buying a subscription to this organisation or checking to see if your literacy co-ordinator or Head of English subscribes. There are lots of good resources here and a huge bank of reports that are directly relevant to reading and schools.
3 The Reading Agency – https://readingagency.org.uk. A charity that has a lot of great information about reading.

A good place for finding the latest information is Twitter. If you are on there, make sure you are following the above websites to ensure you see the latest information. Also, ensure you are following @CILIPInfo and @CILIPSLG as we often retweet articles you will find useful.

School professional review

However informal your review – and schools vary with this – this is an opportunity to mention the training that you would like to undertake during the next year. If it is approved as part of your review by your line manager, then when that opportunity arises you should be able to book on the course with confidence. You can put your Chartership or Certification into your professional review, so that it is documented by the school. Being Chartered won't automatically entitle you to a pay rise, but it should give you more respect and standing in the school.

You are right at the start of your journey to becoming a qualified, professional librarian. It's a great journey and one that I have enjoyed being on myself for many years. There is always something new for the professional to learn and *so much* to learn. Enjoy your journey!

Action points
1 Go to the CILIP website and investigate Chartership and Certification.
2 Investigate some training and get it into your development plan.
3 Do some professional reading and reflect on your own library in light of what you have read.

References

ADHD Foundation (2020) *ADHD Foundation*, www.adhdfoundation.org.uk [accessed 14 February 2022].

Aggleton, J., Carter, C. and Grieve, M. R. (2022) Reading Librarians and School Libraries. In Cremin, T., Hendry, H., Rodriguez Leon, L. and Kucirkova, N. (eds), *Reading Teachers: Nurturing Reading for Pleasure*, Routledge.

All-Party Parliamentary Group for Education (2011) *Report of the Inquiry into Overcoming Barriers to Literacy*, APPG, www.educationengland.org.uk/documents/pdfs/2011-appge-literacy-report.pdf [accessed 14 February 2022].

American Library Association (ALA) Digital Literacy Task Force (2013) ALA Task Force Releases Digital Literacy Recommendations, www.ala.org/news/press-releases/2013/06/ala-task-force-releases-digital-literacy-recommendations [accessed 10 February 2022].

Arain, M., Haque, M., Johal, L., Mathur, P., Nel, W., Rais, A., Sandhu, R. and Sharma, S. (2013) Maturation of the Adolescent Brain, *Neuropsychiatric Disease and Treatment*, **9**, 449–461, https://doi.org/10.2147/NDT.S39776 [accessed 9 February 2022].

ASCEL (n.d.) *SLS UK School Library Award*, www.ascel.org.uk/sls-uk-school-library-award [accessed 14 February 2022].

Ball, S. J. (2000) Performativities and Fabrications in the Education Economy: Towards the Performative Society, *Australian Educational Researcher*, **17** (3), 1–24.

Barratt, L. (2010) Effective School Libraries: Evidence of Impact on Student Achievement, *School Librarian*, **58** (3), 136–9.

Behaviour2Learn (2011) *David Moore Video: The Circle of Intimacy*, www.youtube.com/watch?v=0A-iTNk0Cj4 [accessed 9 February 2022].

Billington, J. (2015) *Reading Between the Lines: The Benefits of Reading for Pleasure*, Quick Reads, University of Liverpool.

Boyes, M. E., Leitao, S., Claessen, M., Badcock, N. A. and Nayton, M. (2016) Why Are Reading Difficulties Associated with Mental Health Problems?, *Dyslexia*, **22** (3), 263–6.

Bush, L. (2002) *Opening Remarks by Mrs Bush at the White House Conference on School Libraries*, White House Press Release, https://georgewbush-whitehouse.archives.gov/news/releases/2002/06/20020604-12.html [accessed 14 February 2022].

Cambridge Dictionary (2022) *Diversity*, https://dictionary.cambridge.org/dictionary/english/diversity [accessed 14 February 2022].

Centre for Literacy in Primary Education (2020) *CLPE Reflecting Realities – Survey of Ethnic Representation within UK Children's Literature*, CLPE, https://clpe.org.uk/research/clpe-reflecting-realities-survey-ethnic-representation-within-uk-childrens-literature [accessed 14 February 2022].

Chema, J. (2018) Adolescents' Enjoyment of Reading as a Predictor of Reading Achievement: New Evidence from a Cross-Country Survey, *Journal of Research in Reading*, **41** (1), 149–62.

CILIP (n.d.) *Impact Toolkit*, www.cilip.org.uk/page/ImpactToolkitImpact5 [accessed 14 February 2022, CILIP membership log-in required].

CILIP ILG (2018) *Definition of Information Literacy*, https://infolit.org.uk/ILdefinitionCILIP2018.pdf [accessed 10 February 2022].

CILIP SLG (n.d.) *To Do Well at School, Every Student Needs a Professional Librarian Who Provides …*, https://cdn.ymaws.com/www.cilip.org.uk/resource/group/d73d9fce-5850-4276-a51f-00d38d6c901c/to_do_well_at_school_leaflet.pdf [accessed 14 February 2022].

CLA (2019) *Cressida Cowell on Being Creative*, CLA Education Blog, 25 September, https://blog.educationplatform.co.uk/2019/09/25/cressida-cowell-on-being-creative [accessed 14 February 2022].

Clark, C. and Teravainen-Goff, A. (2020) *Children and Young People's Reading in 2019: Findings from our Annual Literacy Survey*, National Literacy Trust.

Cowell, C. (2021) *'Libraries Change Lives': Read Cressida Cowell's Open Letter to Prime Minister Boris Johnson*, BookTrust, www.booktrust.org.uk/news-and-features/features/2021/april/libraries-change-lives-read-cressida-cowells-open-letter-to-prime-minister-boris-johnson [accessed 14 February 2022].

Cremin, T., Mottram, M., Powell, S., Collins, R. and Safford, K. (2014) *Building Communities of Engaged Readers*: *Reading for Pleasure*, Routledge.

Cremin, T. and Swann, J. (2017) School Librarians as Facilitators of Extracurricular Reading Groups. In Pihl, J., Skinstad van der Kooij, K. and Carlsten, T. C. (eds), *Teacher and Librarian Partnerships in Literacy Education in the 21st Century*, 118–37, Sense Publishers.

Dempsey, K. (2009) *The Accidental Library Marketer*, Information Today.

Department for Education (DfE) (2014) *The National Curriculum in England: Key Stages 1 and 2*, Crown Copyright, Reference: DFE-00178-2013,

https://assets.publishing.service.gov.uk/government/uploads/system/uploads/attac
hment_data/file/425601/PRIMARY_national_curriculum.pdf.

Department for Education (DfE) (2017) *NFER Teacher Voice Omnibus: Behaviour and
Attendance*, Department for Education,
https://assets.publishing.service.gov.uk/government/uploads/system/uploads/attac
hment_data/file/584503/Teacher_Voice_Summer_2016_Report_Final.pdf [accessed
9 February 2022].

Department for Education (DfE) (2018) *Protection of Biometric Information of Children in
Schools and Colleges*, Department for Education,
https://assets.publishing.service.gov.uk/government/uploads/system/uploads/attac
hment_data/file/692116/Protection_of_Biometric_Information.pdf [accessed 8
February 2022].

Department for Education (DfE) (2021a) *Keeping Children Safe in Education 2021 –
Statutory Guidance for Schools and Colleges*, Department for Education,
https://assets.publishing.service.gov.uk/government/uploads/system/uploads/attac
hment_data/file/1021914/KCSIE_2021_September_guidance.pdf [accessed 8
February 2022].

Department for Education (DfE) (2021b) *National Curriculum*, Department for
Education, www.gov.uk/government/collections/national-curriculum [accessed 10
February 2022].

Department for Education (DfE) (2021c) *Teaching a Broad and Balanced Curriculum for
Education Recovery*, Department for Education,
www.gov.uk/government/publications/teaching-a-broad-and-balanced-
curriculum-for-education-recovery [accessed 14 February 2022].

Department for Education (DfE) (2021d) *The Reading Framework: Teaching and
Foundations of Literacy*, Department for Education,
www.gov.uk/government/publications/the-reading-framework-teaching-the-
foundations-of-literacy [accessed 14 February 2022].

Dewhurst, V. (2021) *Promoting Reading Using the School Library*, SEC ED – The Voice
for Secondary Education, www.sec-ed.co.uk/best-practice/promoting-reading-
using-the-school-library-literacy-books-students-learning-lessons-resources
[accessed 9 February 2022].

Dreikurs, R., Grunwald, B. B. and Pepper, F. C. (2013) *Maintaining Sanity in the
Classroom: Classroom Management Techniques*, Taylor & Francis.

Drew, C. (2021) *79 Examples of School Vision and Mission Statements*,
https://helpfulprofessor.com/school-vision-and-mission-statements [accessed 8
February 2022].

Ee Loh, C., Ellis M., Paculdar, A. A. and Wan, Z. H. (2017) Building a Successful
Reading Culture Through the School Library: A Case Study of a Singapore
Secondary School, *IFLA Journal*, **43** (4), 335–347,
https://doi.org/10.1177/0340035217732069.

Eyre, C. (2021) Childwise Survey Reveals that 25% Never Read for Pleasure, *The Bookseller*, February 12, www.thebookseller.com/news/childwise-survey-reveals-25-never-read-pleasure-1236915# [accessed 14 February 2022].

Galley, K. C. M. (2017) *The Contribution of England's Primary School Libraries to the Development of Students' Information Literacy*, Thesis, Loughborough University, https://hdl.handle.net/2134/24038 [accessed 10 February 2022].

Gibbons, A. (2011) Foreword. In Court, J., *Read to Succeed*, Facet Publishing, ix–x.

Great School Libraries (n.d.) *Why Are School Libraries So Important?*, www.greatschoollibraries.org.uk/about [accessed 14 February 2022].

Great School Libraries (2019) *Great School Libraries Survey Findings and Update on Phase 1*, www.greatschoollibraries.org.uk/_files/ugd/8d6dfb_a1949ea011cd415fbd57a7a0c4471469.pdf [accessed 9 February 2022].

Harris, G. (2021) *Life-changing Libraries*, SLS UK, https://sls-uk.org/response-cressida-cowells-letter [accessed 14 February 2022].

Hartsfield, D. and Kimmel, S. (2020) Supporting the Right to Read: Principles for Selecting Children's Books, *The Reading Teacher*, **74** (4), 419–27.

Hayes, M. (2021) *The DfE's Reading Framework*, Infographic, www.marcrhayes.com/post/the-dfe-s-reading-framework [accessed 14 February 2022].

Howe, J. (2021) *How I Made the School Library the Heart of the School*, https://books2all.co.uk/blog/2021/06/school-library-heart-of-the-school [accessed 9 February 2022].

Humphrey, B. (2021) *Advocacy: Proving Your worth – School Library Advocacy Deck*, SLG Connect, March 15, https://slgconnect.org.uk/2021/03/15/advocacy-proving-your-worth [accessed 14 February 2022].

Jisc (2018) *Quick Guide: Developing Students' Digital Literacy*, https://digitalcapability.jiscinvolve.org/wp/files/2014/09/JISC_REPORT_Digital_Literacies_280714_PRINT.pdf [accessed 10 February 2022].

Kidd, C. D. and Costano, E. (2013) Reading Literary Fiction Improves Theory of the Mind, *Science*, **342** (6156), 377–80.

Kucirkova, N. and Cremin, T. (2017) Personalised Reading for Pleasure with Digital Libraries: Towards a Pedagogy of Practice and Design, *Cambridge Journal of Education*, **48** (5), 571–89, http://dx.doi.org/10.1080/0305764X.2017.1375458.

Lance, K. C. and Kachel, D. E. (2018) Why School Librarians Matter: What Years of Research Tell Us, *Phi Delta Kappan*, **99** (7), 15–20, https://kappanonline.org/lance-kachel-school-librarians-matter-years-research [accessed 14 February 2022].

Lawton, A. (2016) *The Invisible Librarian: A Librarian's Guide to Increasing Visibility and Impact*, Chandos.

Mallette, M. and Barone, D. (2016) Unite for Literacy: An Interview with Mark W. F. Condon, *The Reading Teacher*, **69** (5), 471–81.

Mar, R. A. and Rain, M. (2015) Narrative Fiction and Expository Nonfiction Differentially Predict Verbal Ability, *Scientific Studies of Reading*, **19** (6), 419–33.

Markless, S. and Streatfield, D. (2013) *Evaluating the Impact of Your Library*, 2nd edn, Facet Publishing.

McQuillan, J. (2019) The Inefficiency of Vocabulary Instruction, *International Electronic Journal of Elementary Education*, **11** (4), 309–18.

Mencap (2022) *How Common is Learning Disability?*, www.mencap.org.uk/learning-disability-explained/research-and-statistics/how-common-learning-disability [accessed 14 February 2022].

Merga, M. K. (2017) Becoming a Reader: Significant Social Influences on Avid Book Readers, *School Library Research*, **20**, 1–20.

Merga, M. K. and Mason, S. (2019) Building a School Reading Culture: Teacher Librarians' Perceptions of Enabling and Constraining Factors, *Australian Journal of Education*, **63**, (2), 173–89.

Morpurgo, M. (2009) Let's Get Reading, *The Times*, 17 January, 11–12.

Moses, L. and Kelly, L. B. (2019) Are They Really Reading? A Descriptive Study of First Graders During Independent Reading, *Reading and Writing Quarterly*, **35** (4), 322–38, https://doi.org/10.1080/10573569.2018.1545615.

Moses, L. and Kelly, L. (2018) We're a Little Loud. That's Because We Like to Read!': Developing Positive Views of Reading in a Diverse, Urban First Grade, *Journal of Early Childhood Literacy*, **18** (3), 307–37.

Nakamura, J., Dwight, C. and Shankland, S. (2019) Flow: The Experience of Intrinsic Motivation. In Ryan, R. M. (ed.), *The Oxford Handbook of Human Motivation*, 2nd edn, Oxford Library of Psychology.

National Literacy Trust (2018) *Book Ownership, Literacy Engagement and Mental Wellbeing*, https://literacytrust.org.uk/research-services/research-reports/book-ownership-literacy-engagement-and-mental-wellbeing [accessed 14 February 2022].

National Literacy Trust (NLT) (2021) *What is Literacy?*, https://literacytrust.org.uk/information/what-is-literacy [accessed 10 February 2022].

NHS (2017) *Mental Health of Children and Young People in England, 2017*, https://digital.nhs.uk/data-and-information/publications/statistical/mental-health-of-children-and-young-people-in-england/2017/2017 [accessed 14 February 2022].

NHS Knowledge and Library Services (2021) *What is the Value and Impact Toolkit?*, https://library.hee.nhs.uk/quality-and-impact/value-and-impact/value-and-impact-toolkit [accessed 14 February 2022].

Nootens, P., Morin, M.-F., Alamargot, D., Gonçalves, C., Venet, M. and Labrecque, A.-M. (2019) Differences in Attitudes toward Reading: A Survey of Pupils in Grades 5 to 8, *Frontiers in Psychology*, **9**, 2773, https://doi:10.3389/fpsyg.2018.02773.

OECD (2009) *Pisa 2009 Results: What Students Know and Can Do*, https://doi.org/10.1787/9789264091450-en.

Office for National Statistics (2011) *2011 Census*, www.ons.gov.uk/census/2011census
[accessed 14 February 2022].

Ofsted (2019) *The Education Inspection Framework*,
www.gov.uk/government/publications/education-inspection-framework [accessed
9 February 2022].

Ofsted (2022) *School Inspection Handbook*,
www.gov.uk/government/publications/school-inspection-handbook-eif/school-
inspection-handbook [accessed 14 February 2022].

Oxford English Dictionary (1989) *Plagiarism*, 2nd edn, Clarendon Press.

Patrizio, A. (2018) IDC: Expect 175 zettabytes of data worldwide by 2025,
www.networkworld.com/article/3325397/idc-expect-175-zettabytes-of-data-
worldwide-by-2025.html [accessed 10 February 2022].

Pavey, S. (2005) Bringing the Library to the Classroom: Empowering the Librarian,
ASSIGNATION, **22** (4), 25–30.

Pennac, D. and Blake, Q. (2006) *The Rights of the Reader*,
https://cdn.literacytrust.org.uk/media/documents/HO4_Rights_of_the_reader.pdf
[accessed 8 February 2022].

Primary School Library Guidelines (2022) *What Do You Need?*,
https://primaryschoollibraryguidelines.org.uk/books/selectingresources [accessed 14
February 2022].

Reading Agency (2016) *Reading Outcomes Framework Toolkit*,
https://readingoutcomes.readingagency.org.uk/assets/reports/Outcomes%20Frame
work%20Toolkit_2016_printable_FINAL.pdf [accessed 14 February 2022].

Rudkin, G. and Wood, C. (2019) *Understanding the Impact and Characteristics of School
Libraries and Reading Spaces*, National Literacy Trust.

Scottish Library and Information Council (2018) *Vibrant Libraries, Thriving Schools – A
National Strategy for School Libraries in Scotland 2018–2023*,
https://scottishlibraries.org/media/2110/vibrant-libraries-thriving-schools.pdf
[accessed 14 February 2022].

Seed, A. (2020) *Why Should We Value Factual Books for Children?*,
www.andyseed.com/2020/08/why-should-we-value-factual-books-for-children
[accessed 9 February 2022].

Seed, A. (2021) *How Factual Books Can Get Children Reading*, www.andyseed.com/wp-
content/uploads/2021/04/How-factual-books-can-get-children-reading.pdf
[accessed 9 February 2022].

Sénéchal, M., Hill, S. and Malette, M. (2018) Individual Differences in Grade 4
Children's Written Compositions: The Role of Online Planning and Revising, Oral
Storytelling, and Reading for Pleasure, *Cognitive Development*, **45**, 92–104.

Shaper, S. (ed.) (2014) *The CILIP Guidelines for Secondary School Libraries*, 3rd edn, Facet
Publishing.

SinhaRoy, S. (2016) Data Visualization for the Rest of Us: Tips for Effective Infographics, *American Libraries Magazine*, January 9, https://americanlibrariesmagazine.org/blogs/the-scoop/data-visualization-for-the-rest-of-us [accessed 14 February 2022].

Stanovich, K. E. (1986) Matthew Effects in Reading: Some Consequences of Individual Differences In the Acquisition of Literacy, *Reading Research Quarterly*, **21**, 360–407.

Streatfield, D. and Markless, S. (2022) *Doing Library Impact Evaluation: Enhancing Value and Performance in Libraries*, Facet Publishing.

Suffield, E. (2019) Promoting Reading for Pleasure in School Libraries, SCIS – Schools Catalogue Information Service, Issue 108, Term 1, www.scisdata.com/connections/issue-108/promoting-reading-for-pleasure-in-school-libraries [accessed 9 February 2022].

Sullivan, A. and Brown, M. (2015) Reading for Pleasure and Progress in Vocabulary and Mathematics, *British Educational Research Journal*, **41** (6), 971–91.

Swaen, B. (2021) *Citation Styles Guide: Which Citation Style Should you Use?*, www.scribbr.com/citing-sources/citation-styles [accessed 10 February 2022].

Teravainen, A. and Clark, C. (2017) *School Libraries: A Literature Review of Current Provision and Evidence of Impact*, National Literacy Trust, https://cdn.literacytrust.org.uk/media/documents/2017_06_30_free_research_-_school_library_review_XxR5qcv.pdf [accessed 14 February 2022].

Todd T. T. (2021) *The Future of Primary School Libraries*, National Literacy Trust.

Tower Hamlets SLS (2021) *Library, Information and Research Skills Schemes of Work*, www.towerhamlets-sls.org.uk/infoskills [accessed 14 February 2022].

Twenge, J. M., Campbell, W. K. and Sherman, R. A. (2019) Declines in Vocabulary Among American Adults Within Levels of Educational Attainment, 1974–2016, *Intelligence*, 76, Article 101377

UNESCO (2006) *Alexandria Proclamation on Information Literacy and Lifelong Learning*, www.unesco.org/new/en/communication-and-information/resources/news-and-in-focus-articles/all-news/news/alexandria_proclamation_on_information_literacy_and_lifelong [accessed 10 February 2022].

Williams, A. (2021) *Get Everyone Reading – A Primer on Reading for Pleasure*, SLA, www.sla.org.uk/get-everyone-reading [accessed 8 February 2022].

Williams, D., Wavell, C. and Morrison, K. (2014) Impact of School Libraries on Learning, *Teacher Librarian*, **41** (3), 32.

World Health Organization (2018) *Mental Health: Strengthening Our Response*, www.who.int/news-room/fact-sheets/detail/mental-health-strengthening-our-response [accessed 14 February 2022].

Young Minds (2022) *Mental Health Statistics*, www.youngminds.org.uk/about-us/media-centre/mental-health-statistics [accessed 14 February 2022].

Appendices

Appendix 1: Glossary

Academies: state schools funded directly by the government and run by an academy trust rather than the local authority.

Academy Trust: not-for-profit company who employ the staff and trustees responsible for the performance of schools within the trust.

Accession number: a unique number given to each library resource recorded in the catalogue. This number is often then identified using a barcode.

Advocacy: promoting the worth of an area, such as school librarianship, in general terms.

Alphabetical order: a way of sorting information into A–Z order. Fiction books, for example, can be organised in alphabetical order by the author's last name.

Annual report: yearly report detailing an overview of library activities and finances.

Audio-visual (AV) stock: items you can listen to (audio) or watch (visual).

Barcode: a design consisting of numbers and parallel lines that can be read by machines. Books often have two barcodes: one that identifies the ISBN and book details; the other that identifies the unique accession number.

Benchmarking: to evaluate something by comparison with a standard.

Bibliographic data: data that can be used to identify a book or resource, such as title, author, date of publication, etc.

Book jacket: a strong plastic or sticky-back plastic cover that protects a book. See: Dust jacket.

Book levelling: sorting books into levels according to students' reading abilities. Books are sorted by different coloured labels or a numbering system. Commonly used in primary schools and reading schemes.

Borrow: to take away books or other stock, with the librarian's permission, for a set period of time.

Borrowing system: a method that allows people to take books out of the library for a set period of time. A computerised record of who has borrowed which book helps the librarian to find the book if it is not returned by the specified date.

Branding: the promotion of a product or organisation via advertising and a distinctive design.

Cataloguing: adding details about books and resources to the library catalogue, for example, the author, title, publisher and classification number.

Certification: CILIP Certification is aimed at those who are at the beginning of their professional career or who want to gain some recognition for their knowledge and skills.

Chartership: Chartership is the level of Professional Registration for those working in the information professions who wish to be recognised for their skills, knowledge and application of these in the form of reflective practice.

Classification: the arrangement of resources into groups according to specific criteria, using a classification system such as Dewey.

Classroom library: a collection of books in a classroom for reading by the class based there. May be shelved randomly, organised in broad genres or by book format. Usually managed by the teacher, sometimes by the school librarian. Common in primary schools, whether the school has a central library or not.

Contents: this is a list of the subjects covered in a book. It is usually found at the front of information books and is a useful way of finding out if the book you are looking at has the information you want. It is in chapter order.

Copies: a copy means one book. If you have several books, with the same title and by the same author, then you have multiple copies. Each copy should be given its own unique accession number when cataloguing.

Cross-curricula: across the whole school curriculum.

Curriculum: the study programme for subjects studied in schools.

Data protection: legal control over access to and use of data stored.

Data visualisation: how data is presented, for example, in graph form.

Date stamp: a rubber stamp, used with an ink pad, which can be set to a specific date and used on the return date label.

Demographics: statistical and cultural data relating to the school
community and particular groups within it.

Dewey Decimal Classification System: an international system of library
classification that allows subject identification of resources. Organised by
numbers and decimal points. See also: Simplified Dewey.

Disadvantaged homes: measure of social deprivation or poverty.

Discrimination: unjust treatment of people based on a specific category,
usually race, age, gender or disability.

Diversity: many different types of things or people being included.

Dust jacket: a protective cover for a book, usually made of thick paper.
Hardbacks are often published with dust jackets.

Educational outcomes: the impact on education of initiatives; what
difference the initiative has made to a student's education.

English as an Additional Language (EAL): an EAL student will have a
home language that is not English.

E-portal: another term for intranet.

Extended Project Qualification: this is an A Level standard (Level 3)
standalone qualification.

Facebook: widely used social media.

Feedback: reaction to a product, service, performance, etc., that is used to
improve what is delivered.

Fellowship: Fellowship is the highest level of Professional Registration. It
means your contributions are recognised and valued by a group of your
peers and that you have had an impact on your organisation and wider
profession.

Fiction book: literature created from the imagination.

Footfall: a term used for the measurement of the number of people using a
library.

Form room library: in secondary schools, a way of organising and keeping
books in cupboards in a form room if the school does not have a separate
room for a library. See also: Classroom library.

Free choice: students choose books according to their interests and curiosity.

Further Education: education that occurs after the age of 16 years that
covers all qualifications lower than a degree.

Genre: fiction books of the same type; for example, many authors specialise
in writing one type of book such as mysteries, crime or thrillers.

Hardback: a book with a firm, strong cover, usually more expensive and
not as easily damaged as a paperback book.

Head: Headteacher.

Head of Year: teacher with responsibility for managing a year group within
the school.

Impact: the difference made to stakeholders by actions.

Impact evaluation: a strategy for studying how successful initiatives are by looking at the difference they have made to individuals.

Independent learning/study: students studying independently, for example, in the library by themselves.

Independent schools: fee-paying schools.

Index: an alphabetical list of subjects found in a book, together with page references, usually sited at the back of information books.

Infant schools: schools for children from age 4–7 years, part of primary education. These cover Reception and Key Stage 1 (England and Wales).

Information book: non-fiction book.

Information skills: how to use information for research and writing, part of information literacy.

Instagram: widely used social media app communicating through pictures.

International Baccalaureate: a qualification often taken in private schools instead of A Levels.

International Federation of Library Associations: an international group of libraries with a very useful school libraries sub-division. Great for connecting with international colleagues.

International Standard Book Number (ISBN): a number and barcode which is used to identify a book. This is not the same as your own accession number which is different in each copy. The ISBN is the same in all copies of that book.

Intranet: internal system your school may use to manage all resources in one place, such as Firefly, Glow or SharePoint. Also used for communication, hosting operational systems and as a collaborative platform. It is usually password protected.

Junior schools: schools for children from age 7–11 years, part of primary education covering Key Stage 2 (England and Wales).

Key Stages: divisions by age used in most state schools. Key Stage 1 (KS1) (Years 1 and 2) and Key Stage 2 (KS2) (Years 3 to 6) cover primary schools. Key Stage 3 (KS3) (Years 7 to 9) and Key Stage 4 (KS4) (Years 10 and 11) cover secondary schools. KS5 (Years 12 and 13) is also known as Sixth Form.

Kinderboxes: book storage designed for picture books to facilitate access by small children. Books are stored front cover forward to allow easy access for young children.

Library committee: A small decision-making group chosen from the school community.

Library Development Plan: this is a plan which is produced by you to integrate with the School Development Plan. It guides you through the next year/few years in planning your library.

Library handbook: explanation of library policies and contains specific actions to be taken in certain circumstances.

Library management system: This is a computer system which is used to run the multiple functions of the library: cataloguing, issuing, returning, making lists, identifying stock, stocktaking, etc.

Library supplier: a company that specialises in providing books, stationery and other equipment for libraries.

Library users: people who visit the library.

Line manager: person with direct managerial responsibility for the librarian.

LIPSSEE: Librarians in Independent Prep Schools in the South East of England – a support organisation for school librarians.

Literacy: the ability to read, write, listen and speak. In primary schools, the teaching of reading skills and literature.

Literacy co-ordinator: the person responsible for managing literacy teaching and initiatives in a school.

Literacy lead: same as Literacy co-ordinator. Usually used in primary schools.

Loan/lend: To allow library users to borrow books for a set period of time.

Marketing: encompasses all the activities undertaken to promote and advertise products and services provided by the library.

Mission statement: a formal statement of values and objectives. It defines the ethos, goals and purpose of the school and/or library.

National Curriculum: a programme of study within schools in England that is designed to ensure conformity of standards and content.

Neurodiversity: a range of variations in the brain regarding sociability, learning, attention, mood and other mental functions.

Nursery schools: can also be known as pre-school, for children aged 3–4. May be publicly or privately operated (England and Wales).

Objectives: what activities or events are trying to achieve.

Office for Standards in Education, Children's Services and Skills (Ofsted): inspection body for state schools and other educational settings.

Oversize book: a large book that does not fit on to standard size bookshelves.

Pastoral team: staff who provide for the physical and emotional welfare of students, particularly those with special educational needs, disabilities or mental health issues.

Periodical: another name for a magazine.

Portable Document Format (PDF): a format to save a document on a word processing package so that the reader is unable to alter it.

Preparatory (prep) schools: independent fee-paying schools for students aged 4 to 11 years or 4 to 13 years.

Pre-school: see Nursery schools.

Primary schools: schools for students aged 4 to 11 years, covering Reception, Key Stage 1 and Key Stage 2

Project box/subject file: a box or file in which a variety of stock about the same subject, for example, the environment, is stored. A project box is a good place to keep pamphlets and small booklets that might not be easy to see on bookshelves. Also known as a 'topic box' in primary schools.

Promotion: advertising particular activities, events and initiatives.

Public schools: fee-paying schools. Can either be day or boarding schools, or a mixture of both. Also known as independent schools.

Publication date: the date when a book is published. It is usually found on the back of the title page.

Publisher: a company that produces books or magazines and other resources.

Pupil library assistant (PLA): a student who helps in the library on a voluntary basis, maybe as part of a team.

Pupil premium: grant designed to allow schools to help disadvantaged students by improving their progress and exam results. Students are eligible for a number of reasons – family income or occupation (children whose parents are in the Armed Forces are automatically PP students), children in care, eligible for free school meals at any time in the last six years (known as Ever 6).

Qualitative data: non-numerical data that describes information or a characteristic. It is usually collected via questionnaires and interviews.

Quantitative data: statistical data in the form of numbers or measurements.

Quarterly: a way of describing something that is done four times a year. Some magazines, for example, are published every three months – four times a year.

RADAR: Rationale, Authority, Date, Accuracy, Relevance. A framework for recognising source text reliability and validity.

Reading for pleasure: reading books for interest rather than study.

Reference book: an information book where students and staff can find quick answers and which cannot be borrowed from the library.

Reluctant readers: students who show little interest in reading books. This may be because of a learning difficulty, illiteracy, low self-esteem, not being shown books they enjoy or some other reason.

Reprint: a further edition of a book, produced by the publisher when the initial number of copies printed has sold out.

Return date label: a label in the front of the book where the date by which a borrowed book must be returned to the library is written or stamped.

Routine: a task that is done regularly.

Scheme of Work (SoW): a plan that outlines the learning to be covered over a given period of time. It defines the structure and content of an academic course.

School community: students, teaching staff, support staff, peripatetic staff, senior leaders, governors, parents/carers.

School Development Plan (SDP): strategic document that determines objectives and targets of the schools and is used for raising standards. See also: School Improvement Plan.

School Improvement Plan: alternative term for School Development Plan.

School inspectorate: a formal body for inspecting independent or non-local authority run state schools, such as academies or free schools, to ensure their adherence to national standards.

School library policy: a framework for the operation of the library explaining its purpose and main functions.

Schools Library Service (SLS): usually a subscription-based library organisation supporting schools with regular loans of books and other resources, advice about planning and running school libraries, and, sometimes, supplying experienced/qualified librarians to run the school's library.

Secondary schools: schools for students aged 11–16 years, covering Key Stage 3 and 4, or 11–18 years, covering Key Stage 3, 4 and 5.

Self-evaluation: the process of analysing and evaluating the effectiveness of one's own work.

Shelf guide: a sign that shows library users where resources are kept on the bookshelves.

Simplified Dewey: Dewey Decimal Classification using three numbers and no or infrequent decimal points. Usually used in primary schools, sometimes in combination with a coloured label to indicate the broad subject.

Sole (or solo) librarian: a librarian working alone with no other library staff.

Special educational needs (SEN): a legal definition that refers to children with learning difficulties or disabilities.

Special educational needs and disabilities (SEND): a legal definition that refers to children with special educational needs (learning difficulties or disabilities) and physical disabilities.

Spine: the backbone of a book. If the spine is broken, the book's pages and cover may fall apart.

Spine label: a label stuck to a book's spine so that you can quickly identify the subject area of the book or author and where it should be kept on the bookshelves.

Stakeholders: the individuals or community affected by the library strategy.
State schools: schools funded by the government, sometimes directly by them, sometimes via a local authority, and open to everyone. Free of charge. Includes LA (local authority) schools, free schools, academies, some special schools and some faith schools.
Statutory: required by law.
Stocktake: a method of checking to see what stock is in the library.
Strategic management: managing the whole strategy in the long term.
Subject index: an alphabetical list of the subjects covered by the resources in the library and their classification. The subject index is useful to remind students of the main subjects in the library and their classification codes.
SWOT analysis: a strategy for identifying Strengths, Weaknesses, Opportunities and Threats.
Through-schools: schools for students aged 3–18 years.
Title page: the page at the front of a book that has the title, author and, sometimes, publisher printed on it.
Title verso page: a left-hand page near the front of a book containing information about the book, for example, publisher, date published, copyright details, etc.
Twitter: widely used social media app, with short 280-character limit.
United Kingdom Literacy Association (UKLA): an organisation that supports teachers with literacy teaching.
Vision: what the service is aiming to achieve.
Weeding: removing out-of-date or damaged books from the library.
Wikipedia: online, open source, free to use encyclopedia.
Youth Libraries Group (YLG): CILIP group that includes members from schools, public libraries, Schools Library Services and others working with young people.

Appendix 2: National Book Initiatives
Holocaust Memorial Day
Takes place on 27 January
www.hmd.org.uk

LGBT+ History Month
Takes place in February
https://lgbtplushistorymonth.co.uk

Safer Internet Day
Takes place in February
www.saferinternetday.org

Harry Potter Book Night
Takes place in February
www.bloomsbury.com/uk/discover/harry-potter/harry-potter-book-night/harry-potter-book-night.

World Book Day
Takes place on the first Thursday in March
www.worldbookday.com

International Women's Day
Takes place annually on 8 March
www.internationalwomensday.com

British Science Week
Takes place in March
www.britishscienceweek.org

National Share-A-Story Month
Takes place in May
https://fcbg.org.uk/nssm

Empathy Day
Takes place in June
www.empathylab.uk

Summer Reading Challenge
Takes place during the school summer holidays
https://summerreadingchallenge.org.uk

National Poetry Day
Takes place on the first Thursday in October
https://nationalpoetryday.co.uk

Black History Month
Takes place during October
www.blackhistorymonth.org.uk

National Non-Fiction November
Takes place throughout the whole of November
https://fcbg.org.uk/nnfn

Appendix 3: National Book Awards

Blue Peter Book Awards
www.bbc.co.uk/cbbc/watch/bp-book-awards

Branford Boase Award
https://branfordboaseaward.org.uk

Costa Book Awards
www.costa.co.uk/behind-the-beans/costa-book-awards/book-awards

FCBG Children's Book Award
https://fcbg.org.uk/childrens-book-award

Little Rebels Award
https://littlerebels.org

Lollies Laugh Out Loud
https://shop.scholastic.co.uk/lollies/about

Sainsbury's Children's Book Awards
www.booktrust.org.uk/what-we-do/awards-and-prizes/current-prizes/Sainsburys-childrens-book-awards

SLA Information Book Award
www.sla.org.uk/information-book-award

UKLA Book Awards
https://ukla.org/awards/ukla-book-award

Waterstones's Children's Book Prize
www.waterstones.com/category/cultural-highlights/book-awards

YA Book Prize
www.thebookseller.com/awards/awards/the-ya-book-prize

Yoto Carnegie and Kate Greenaway Medals
https://carnegiegreenaway.org.uk

Appendix 4: Links to Information Literacy Models
5As
Macdonald, B., Dosaj, A., Jukes, I. (2000) *NetSavvy: Building Information Literacy in the Classroom*, SAGE Publications.
5E Inquiry Model (Bybee)
Bybee, R. W. (2009) *The BSCS 5E Instructional Model and 21st Century Skills*, NABSE.
8Ws (Lamb)
Lamb, A., Smith, N., and Johnson, L. (1997) Wondering, Wiggling, and Weaving: A New Model for Project and Community-Based Learning on the Web, *Learning and Leading with Technology*, **24**, 7–13.
Alberta Learning Inquiry Model
Alberta Learning (2004) *Focus on Inquiry: A Teacher's Guide to Implementing Inquiry-Based Learning*, Learning and Teaching Resources Branch.
BAT (younger students – simplified PSU)
Nesset, V. (2015) Using Empirical Data to Refine a Model for Information Literacy Instruction for Elementary School Students. In *Proceedings of ISIC, the Information Behaviour Conference*, Leeds, 2–5 September 2014: Part 2 (paper isicsp14), http://InformationR.net/ir/20-1/isic2/isicsp14.html.
BIG 6 (Eisenberg & Berkowitz)
The Big6 (2021) *The Big6 and the Super3*, https://thebig6.org/thebig6andsuper3-2.
Empire State Information Fluency Continuum (ESIFC) (Stripling)
Stripling, B. (2021) *Empire State Information Fluency Continuum*, https://slsa-nys.libguides.com/ifc.
FLIP IT (Yucht)
Yucht, A. H. (1997) *Flip It! An Information Skills Strategy for Student Researchers*, Linworth Publishing.
FOSIL (Toerien) (UK adapted version of ESIFC)
Toerien, D. (2021) *The FOSIL Group*, https://fosil.org.uk.
Humanities Model of Inquiry (Bateman)
Bateman, D. (2014) Developing Teachers of Inquiry: An Emerging Humanities Model of Inquiry (HMI), *Ethos*, **22** (1), 8–11.
I-Learn (Neuman et al.)
Neuman, D., Teece DeCarlo, M. J., Lee, V. J., Greenwell, S. and Grant, A. (2019) *Learning in Information-Rich Environments: I-LEARN and the Construction of Knowledge from Information*, 2nd edn, Springer.

I-Search (Macrorie)
Macrorie, K. (1988) *The I-Search Paper*, Boynton/Cook Publishers.
Imposed Query (Gross)
Gross, M. (1999) Imposed Queries in the School Library Media Center: A Descriptive Study, *Library & Information Science Research*, **21** (4), 501–21.
Information Search Process (ISP) (Kuhlthau)
Kuhlthau, C., Maniotes, L. K. and Caspari, A. K. (2007) *Guided Inquiry: Learning in the 21st Century*, Libraries Unlimited.
Inquiry Cycle (Gourley)
Gourley, B. (2008) Inquiry: The Road Less Traveled, *Knowledge Quest*, **37** (1), 18–23.
Irvings (Irving)
Irving, A. (1985) *Study and Information Skills Across the Curriculum*, Heinemann Educational Books.
NoodleTools (Abilock)
Abilock, D. (2021) *NoodleTools*, www.noodletools.com.
Pathways to Knowledge (Pappas & Tepe)
Pappas, M. L. and Tepe, A. E. (2002) *Pathways to Knowledge and Inquiry Learning*, Libraries Unlimited.
PLUS (Herring)
Herring, J. E. (2004) *The Internet and Information Skills*, Facet Publishing.
Pre-search (Rankin)
Rankin, V. (1999) *The Thoughtful Researcher: Teaching the Research Process to Middle School Students*, Libraries Unlimited.
Problem Based Learning (McMaster University)
Hung, W., Jonassen, D. H., and Liu, R. (2007) Problem-Based Learning. In Spector, J. M., van Merriënboer, J. G., Merrill, M. D. and Driscoll, M. (eds.) *Handbook of Research on Educational Communications and Technology*, 3rd edn, Lawrence Erlbaum Associates, 1503–81.
PSU (Nesset)
Nesset, V. (2013) Two Representations of the Research Process: The Preparing, Searching, and Using (PSU) and the Beginning, Acting and Telling (BAT) models, *Library and Information Science Research*, **35** (2), 97–106.
REACTS (Stripling & Pitts)
Stripling, B. and Pitts, J. (1988) *Brainstorms and Blueprints: Teaching Research as a Thinking Process*, Libraries Unlimited.
Research Cycle (McKenzie)
McKenzie, J. (2000) *Beyond Technology: Questioning, Research, and the Information Literate School*, FNO Press.
Science Technology Society (STS) Inquiry Model (Joyce & Weil)
Joyce, G. and Weil, M. (1986) *Models of Teaching*, Prentice-Hall.

Scientific Method

Gimbel, S. (2011) *Exploring the Scientific Method*, University of Chicago Press.

Simple Four (Alewine)

Alewine, M. (2006) *Overview of the Simple Four: An Information Problem-Solving Model*, http://icts-sc.pbworks.com/w/page/10507141/The Simple Four.

Suchman Inquiry Model

Suchman, J. R. (1966) A Model for the Analysis of Inquiry. In Klausmeier, J. and W. Harris, C. W. (eds), *Analysis of Concept Learning*, Academic Press.

Super 3 (younger students – simplified BIG 6) (Eisenberg & Berkowitz)

The Big6 (2021) *The Big6 and the Super3*, https://thebig6.org/thebig6andsuper3-2.

WebQuests (Dodge)

WebQuests (2021) *Home Page*, https://webquest.org.

Zoom In Inquiry

Zoom In (2021) *Home Page*, http://zoomin.edc.org.

Appendix 5: Links to Digital Literacy Models

Belshaw, D. (2014) *The Essential Elements of Digital Literacies*, www.frysklab.nl/wp-content/uploads/2016/10/The-Essential-Elements-of-Digital-Literacies-v1.0.pdf.

Hague, C. and Payton, S. (2010) *FutureLab Handbook: Digital Literacy Across the Curriculum*, www.nfer.ac.uk/publications/FUTL06/FUTL06.pdf.

Jenkins, H. et al. (2006) *Confronting the Challenges of a Participatory Culture: Media Education for the 21st Century*, www.macfound.org/media/article_pdfs/jenkins_white_paper.pdf.

Appendix 6: Links to Evaluation of Information Models

Blakeslee, S. (2004) The CRAAP Test, *LOEX Quarterly*, **31**, 6–7.

Caulfield, M. A. (2017) *Web Literacy for Student Fact-Checkers*, Pressbooks, https://webliteracy.pressbooks.com. (Covers SIFT – Four Moves).

Mandalios, J. (2013) RADAR: An Approach for Helping Students Evaluate Internet Sources, *Journal of Information Science*, **39** (4), 470–8, https://doi.org/10.1177/0165551513478889.

Radom, R. and Gammons, R. W. (2014) Teaching Information Evaluation with the 5 Ws: An Elementary Method, An Instructional Scaffold, and the Effect on Student Recall and Application, *Reference & User Services Quarterly*, **53** (4), 334–47.

Appendix 7: Organisations Supporting Primary Schools and Primary School Librarians

Primary School Library Guidelines: explains how to set up and run a primary school library. Essential reading.
https://primaryschoollibraryguidelines.org.uk.

Librarians in Prep Schools in South East England (LIPSSEE): prep school librarians can join for networking, training and support. Anyone can join, with no geographical limits. https://preplibs.wordpress.com.

Schools Library Services (SLSs): Schools subscribe to their nearest SLS to receive loans of topic books and fiction in all genres and support from trained librarians. SLS librarians may offer visits to the school to establish and maintain the library. Some SLSs only support primary schools. SLS UK can advise further. https://SLS-UK.org.

Centre for Literacy in Primary Education (CLPE): core book lists of key texts by age, a library of children's books, Power of Reading and other training courses, and literacy resources. https://clpe.org.uk.

Chatterbooks: this reading initiative is run by The Reading Agency and is aimed at primary school reading clubs. It suggests books by theme and offers free sets of books. https://readingagency.org.uk/children/quick-guides/chatterbooks.

Books for Topics: search for books for primary school curriculum topics. www.booksfortopics.com.

Appendix 8: Literacy Organisations for Primary and Secondary Schools

The **United Kingdom Literacy Association (UKLA)** informs people interested in language, literacy and communication in all its forms, including literacy learning and teaching. https://ukla.org/about.

The **National Literacy Trust (NLT)** is a charity working with schools and communities to help disadvantaged children with literacy skills. https://literacytrust.org.uk.

The **Reading Agency** works with children and adults to develop reading. https://readingagency.org.uk.

Letterbox Library – multicultural diversity children's books. www.letterboxlibrary.com.

BookTrust offers a 'bookfinder' feature on its website, Book Buzz (schools buy specially chosen books at low cost to give free to new Year 7 students) and Bookstart (free books offered to families of pre-school children) and other projects. www.booktrust.org.uk.

Empathy Lab produces reading lists for primary and secondary schools on books encouraging empathy and organises the annual Empathy Day. www.empathylab.uk.

The Federation of Children's Book Groups has local book groups and runs National Share-A-Story Month and Non-Fiction November. https://fcbg.org.uk.

The **School Library Association (SLA)** offers online training, research, publications and other resources. www.sla.org.uk.

CILIP School Libraries Group (SLG) offers professional publications, support, information resources and training courses to all school librarians. www.cilip.org.uk/members/group_content_view.asp?group=201313&id=687966.

School Librarians' Network is an online forum supporting UK school librarians. https://groups.io/g/SLN.

Appendix 9: Selected Sources of Information about Children's Books

LoveReading4Kids: search for books by ages 7+, 9+ and 11+. www.lovereading4kids.co.uk.

ReadingZone: www.readingzone.com

Pen and Inc: magazine published by CILIP, promoting diversity in children's books publishing. www.cilip.org.uk/page/penandinc.

Books for Keeps: online children's book magazine. http://booksforkeeps.co.uk.

Toppsta: book reviews and recommendations. https://toppsta.com.

The School Librarian: magazine, including articles, features and book reviews by age from Early Years to 16+. www.sla.org.uk/the-school-librarian.

Selected library book suppliers for primary and secondary schools:

Peters: https://peters.co.uk
Browns Books for Schools: www.brownsbfs.co.uk
Heath Educational Books: www.heathbooks.co.uk
Their websites are useful for keeping up to date with new books.

Appendix 10: Approximate Comparison of Education Phases in the Devolved Nations

Age in years	England and Wales: National Curriculum plus Foundation Stage in Wales	Scotland: Curriculum for Excellence	Northern Ireland: Northern Ireland Curriculum
4/5	Reception – Early Years – EYFS	Nursery Early Level	Year 1
5/6	Year 1 Key Stage 1	P1 Early Level	Year 2
6/7	Year 2	P2 First Level	Year 3
7/8	Year 3 Key Stage 2	P3	Year 4
8/9	Year 4	P4	Year 5
9/10	Year 5	P5 Second Level	Year 6
10/11	Year 6	P6	Year 7
11/12	Year 7 Key Stage 3	P7	Year 8
12/13	Year 8	S1 Third/Fourth Level	Year 9
13/14	Year 9	S2	Year 10
14/15	Year 10 Key Stage 4	S3	Year 11
15/16	Year 11	S4 Senior Phase	Year 11
16/17	Year 12 Key Stage 5	S5	Year 13 Sixth Form
17/18	Year 13	S6	Year 14

Index